THE
SOUL'S RISING

DISCLAIMER

Copyright © 2026 by Sarah Jayd
First published in 2026. All rights reserved.
Published by **Oracle Queen Publishing**
www.oraclequeenpublishing.com

No part of this book may be reproduced, stored, or transmitted in any form or by any means — electronic, mechanical, photocopying, recording, or otherwise — without prior written permission from the publisher, except for brief quotations (under 10%) used in reviews, articles, or other non-commercial purposes as permitted under copyright law.

The views, experiences, and perspectives shared within this book belong to the individual contributors and are expressed from their own lived experience. They do not necessarily reflect the views of the editor or publisher. This book is offered as a collection of personal stories, not as a unified belief system or doctrine.

The information shared in this book is provided for general purposes only and is not intended as professional, financial, medical, or legal advice. Readers are encouraged to use their own discernment and seek appropriate support or guidance relevant to their individual circumstances.

While every effort has been made to ensure accuracy, neither the contributors, editor, nor the publisher accept responsibility for errors, omissions, or outcomes arising from the use of this material. The contributors, editor, and publisher disclaim any liability for direct or indirect loss or consequences resulting from the application of information contained within this book.

Every individual's experience is unique, and outcomes may vary. By reading and engaging with this book, you acknowledge and accept full responsibility for your own interpretations, choices, and actions.

Publisher: Oracle Queen Publishing
Publishing Support, Production Oversight and Curation: Sarah Jayd
ISBN: 978-1-7638270-5-9
For distribution or rights inquiries: publishing@oraclequeenpublishing.com

About Oracle Queen Publishing: *An independent publishing house devoted to supporting creators and authors on their self-publishing journey. We believe every storyteller deserves the tools, guidance, and confidence to bring their work to life. From concept to completion, we offer high-touch support, creative direction, and professional expertise, empowering authors to publish independently while retaining full ownership of their work.*

www.oraclequeenpublishing.com

ABOUT THE PUBLISHER

I create collaborative books because I believe stories are medicine when they are shared with honesty and care. I am deeply committed to creating spaces where voices are not rushed, edited into shape, or asked to perform — but are allowed to arrive as they are. This work matters to me because lived experience carries wisdom, and when it is witnessed, it reminds others they are not alone.

As the publisher and curator of this book, my role has been to hold the container for these stories — to gather, guide, and gently weave them together with integrity. Each contributor was invited to share from their own truth, in their own voice. My responsibility has been to honour those truths, protect the space, and ensure this book feels safe, respectful, and intentional for both the writers and the readers.

My hope is that as you move through these pages, you feel met rather than instructed. That something within you softens, remembers, or breathes a little easier. Take what resonates, leave what doesn't, and trust your own inner knowing as you engage with the words offered here.

Sarah Jayd

Oracle Queen Publishing

Some stories in this book explore sensitive life experiences. Please read with self-care and compassion for yourself.

HOW TO READ THIS BOOK

This book is not meant to be rushed.

It has been created as a collection of lived experiences, each shared in its own voice and rhythm. You are not required to read these stories in any particular order, nor to take them all in at once. You are invited to move through the pages in a way that feels supportive, intuitive, and aligned for you.

Some chapters may resonate immediately. Others may gently wait until a later moment in your life. Trust that every story belongs here, and that your inner knowing will guide which words meet you now — and which may return to you another time.

As you read, notice what arises in your body, your breath, and your awareness. If you feel moved to pause, reflect, or ground yourself, honour that instinct. This book is not going anywhere. Your wellbeing matters more than momentum.

Each contribution is offered as lived experience, not instruction. These stories are not here to teach you what to think, believe, or do — they are here to be witnessed. Let them sit beside you rather than lead you, and allow your own insights to unfold naturally.

Toward the end of each chapter, you'll find ways to learn more about the contributor if you feel called. These details are shared simply as points of connection — not expectation. If a story resonates and you wish to explore that voice further, you are welcome to reach out in your own time and way.

There is no obligation to do so. Take what resonates, leave what doesn't, and trust yourself as you engage with the words offered here.

This book meets you where you are.

contents

Chapter 01	**Where Silence Speaks, Freedom Breathes** *Leanne Cathro*	08
Chapter 02	**Remembering Who I Have Always Been** *Kerryn Slater*	26
Chapter 03	**From the Dust Comes Beauty** *Linda Usope*	40
Chapter 04	**The Woman Who Walks Between Worlds** *Jo Rolfe*	50
Chapter 05	**Awakening From My Deep Slumber** *Korinna Zoya Hunter*	64
Chapter 06	**From Grief to Grace** *Sarah Jane Michaels*	76
Chapter 07	**Dimensions and Timelines Through the Eyes of Self** *Carola Werth*	88
Chapter 08	**When Spirit Entered My Life and Cracked Me Open** *Melissa Paris*	100
Chapter 09	**They Never Stopped Talking** *Meg Evans-Blair*	112
Chapter 10	**Crisis as Catalyst: When Love Became the Initiation** *Joergette Mae Medel*	124
Chapter 11	**The Woman with Wings She Didn't Know She Had** *Liz Mulheron*	136
Chapter 12	**When Your Soul Chooses Itself** *Michelle Wollaston*	148

contributors

contributors

CAROLA WERTH

MELISSA PARIS

MEG EVANS-BLAIR

JOERGETTE MAE MEDEL

LIZ MULHERON

MICHELLE WOLLASTON

chapter 01

Where Silence Speaks, Freedom Breathes

by Leanne Cathro

Since I was a little girl, I always sensed there was more to this world than what my eyes could see. At night, lying in bed, I would feel a presence. Sometimes it hovered by the window, sometimes at the corner of my bed, but it was always nearby. At first, it frightened me. The unknown was uncomfortable, I finally mustered up the courage to talk about what I was sensing, it was quickly dismissed.

"Spirits aren't real," they told me.

"You just have an overactive imagination."

But deep inside, I knew it was not my imagination.

Even in church, my body often told me something different from what the pastor was saying. A heaviness sat in my chest when I listened to sermons about sin, shame, and fear. I remember asking questions no one seemed able — or willing — to answer:

If God is love, why would He make us feel ashamed of who we are?

If we are made in His image, why would He want us to live in fear of Hell?

The answers never satisfied me. Fear-based teachings did not feel light or true in my body. Even as a child, I could sense when something was not aligned with love. To me, 'Hell' never seemed like a fiery pit in some faraway place. Hell was already here, on this earth — in the suffering, cruelty, and disconnection people lived with every day.

We live in a world that often rewards bad behaviour — a system that is unfair, distorts truth, and rewards lies, shaping how we see reality. It can make us feel stuck, small, and powerless. But your truth cannot be contained. You naturally have an inner knowing, a deep sense of what is real. Even when the world seems to favour deception, standing in your clarity and honouring what feels true for you creates freedom. Your voice, your choices, and your awareness are stronger than any system — they are the forces that shape your reality.

"Core values are the guiding principles that shape your decisions, behaviour, and the life you create. They reflect what truly matters to you — your sense of integrity, purpose, and what you stand for."

And so, I began to doubt people, what they would say, and their intentions. I would notice what felt heavy. It is not that I did not believe in God, I did not trust the teachings were true for me.

This is not just about religion; it is about what we have been taught from society. What's socially acceptable and belief systems.

Growing up, I was taught that children should be seen and not heard. At first, it seemed like just a phrase adults threw around. But those words carved themselves into me so deeply that I began to live as though my thoughts were unimportant, my voice carried no value, and my feelings were something to be ashamed of. Feeling invisible like I'm watching from the outside looking in.

I told myself: What I say isn't important. My presence does not matter. My truth does not belong here.

That one belief planted a seed of self-doubt that grew wild in my life for years to come.

My instincts would whisper, but I would silence them with endless "What ifs?" and "Maybe I'm wrong." I gave and forgave until my heart was raw. People became so used to me being the one who never said no, the one who always bent, that when I finally started to say "enough," I was suddenly the problem.

I did talk in love but naively, I would tell myself they did not do that on purpose. That was my innocence and I wondered why they would use that against me. Innocence is a beautiful thing. We are not born street smart. That comes from a lived experience when we are betrayed by the most unexpected people.

Suddenly I had a car accident and went under the tray of a ute. I went into shock. I felt cold and alone.

Not long after this I started having flash backs of things that happened when I was very young. I questioned if it could be real, so I spoke to my Nonna who confirmed they actually happened.

"I have been wondering how things like this can happen without you having any memory of them until much later. People say the mind blocks out certain experiences as a survival mechanism to protect us. When the memories finally resurface, it can make you feel like you are losing your grip and question why these thoughts are suddenly coming up now."

Visions come to us as messages — often as pictures, followed by words and feelings.

They invite awareness.

Through sacred breath, we learn how to stay present.

We grow and change one thought at a time.

Things are not always what they seem.

Perception shapes our reality.

Our souls plan experiences so we can learn from them.

Every experience holds wisdom.

Our journey is powerful.

Awakening is a remembering — some call it an Akashic awakening or Akashic records.

Old paradigms from past experiences begin to change.

Spiritual families remain connected.

We are often led intuitively, especially as women, drawing teachings from many sources — not needing recognition or validation from the outside.

Way-showers simply show the way.

As old souls, we remember for a reason.

True power comes from being comfortable with yourself, fully accepting who you are.

The invitation is always there — to awaken and to know who you are.

Awakening is a return to self.

A compassionate, loving knowing.

It arrives in "aha" moments of recognition.

You consciously choose to change your way of thinking for your own greater good.

As your understanding grows and shifts, this is what awakening is.

You come into a new reality — a new way of being and thinking.

When I first started to learn how to become fully present, I realised that I had been in fact 'leaving my body' when I felt stressed.

Not hovering, not leaving to explore, but withdrawing to survive.

Awareness does not float above; it folds inward, tucks itself somewhere unreachable. The world keeps moving, but you are no longer available to it. Sensation dulls, emotion goes flat or distant, not because you do not feel, but because feeling would cost too much. So the system chooses quiet.

It is not absence as in gone. It is absence as in protected.

A strategic disappearance.

Nothing mystical about it, really — just the mind saying: this is too much right now, I'll be back when it's safer. And when you return, there's often that strange aftertaste: time skipped, memories fuzzy, the sense you were there and not there at once.

This is common during trauma; it's often described as dissociation — a protective response where the nervous system reduces conscious awareness to survive overwhelming threat. In moments when escape is impossible and fear or pain exceeds what the mind can process, attention disconnects from sensation, emotion, and sometimes identity itself.

This is why traumatic events can feel unreal while they are happening, as if observed from far away or not experienced at all.

Memory encoding depends on presence, safety, and integration; when the brain shifts into survival mode, it prioritises keeping the body alive over forming coherent memories.

As a result, experiences may be stored in fragments — sensations without stories, emotions without timelines, or gaps where memory should be.

This loss is not forgetting by choice but a biological interruption: awareness was deliberately withdrawn to protect what could not yet be endured. Understanding this helps reframe memory gaps not as weakness or denial, but as evidence of how fiercely the mind and body worked to keep the person alive. Bringing awareness back later must happen slowly and safely, because what was hidden away was hidden for a reason.

When I became aware of this, I chose to stay.

I learned to face my fears, remain present in my body, and make conscious choices that honoured me.

I learned to trust my own knowing.

By staying with myself, I found safety within.

I stopped abandoning myself.

I returned to my role as a wisdom keeper — simply being, with compassion and love.

And then came the night that broke me open.

Hands wrapped around my throat, and my life flashed before my eyes. Time slowed, and every memory rushed past me in blinding speed. In that terrifying stillness, I made a choice. I chose to live.

And in that choice, I saw something clearly: losing everything was not the loss I thought it would be. It was the beginning of gaining something much greater — myself.

Respect had to start with me. I had to learn how to stand with myself, how to forgive myself for abandoning my own needs, and how to hold myself with the same love I so freely gave to others. It was easier to love others than to love myself — that was the hardest truth of all. But admitting it, meant I could finally change.

The day I realised I had not truly had my own back was the day I began to rise.

Long before I lost my Nonna, Spirit had already begun whispering to me in dreams.

I would dream of things happening to loved ones, and days later they would unfold in waking life exactly as I had seen them. At first, I thought it was a coincidence, but the details were too precise to ignore.

I remember one dream about my brother with startling clarity. In the dream, I saw his head split open from a rock. I told my mum, not thinking much of it, but my brother overheard. He laughed, called me a freak, then lifted his hair to reveal the wound — the very injury I had described. My blood ran cold. How could I have seen this days before it happened?

I carried those dreams like a secret, unsure what to do with them. Was I being shown the future to change it? Or only to witness, or trust my own knowing. I did not know.

All I knew was that my dreams were no longer just dreams.

My brother, in his own way, understood. He could see things others could not. His courage gave me a mirror: I was not alone.

And then there was Nonna. She too had the gift of dreaming. She would see things before they happened, and they always came true. "If your Nonna says it will happen, it will happen," my Nonno used to say. I did not realise it then, but she had been showing me all along what it meant to trust the unseen.

When she passed, my heart broke. She had been more than a

grandmother; she had been like a mother, present for every milestone, every first. Her absence cut me raw.

And yet — she found her way back to me.

Her voice began filling my mind, rapid, unmistakable, exactly as she spoke in life. I wondered at first if grief had made me imagine it. But the truth rang louder than doubt: it was her. Nonna was proving to me that death is not the end.

Her visits came when I needed them most, reminding me that the veil between this world and the next is not as thick as we think.

Not long after, another wave of loss arrived.

While driving to a healing class, my grandmother's voice came through again. She told me, clear as anything, that my Nonno would soon leave this world. Tears blurred my eyes as I gripped the steering wheel. I knew in my bones it was true.

So I began to prepare — not in dread, but in presence. I spent time with him, making memories that would outlive the sorrow. One night, we went to a comedy show. Big mistake. The comedian spent most of the set joking about his gay life. My elderly, old-fashioned grandfather leaned over, thick Italian accent and all, and said, "You're joking — this is disgusting!" I laughed so hard I snorted. "Welcome to 2020," I said. I should have checked the content before booking, but he just shrugged and went with the flow like the champ he was. That is who he was; always full of surprises, always finding joy, always making the world a little lighter. We talked about gut feelings, we laughed until our cheeks hurt, and I cherished every single visit.

As his death drew closer and he did not want to leave the house, I found it hard to know what to say. Sadness began to take hold, quietly creeping in, making every moment feel heavier.

When the time came, his final words carved themselves into me. He prayed the Lord's Prayer in Italian, trembling but strong, each syllable a farewell. He told us he was sorry to leave, but excited to see his wife again. His grief and his joy lived in the same breath.

THE SOUL'S RISING

I couldn't bring myself to see him in his final decline. Instead, I held onto the memory of his strength. I delivered his eulogy, something I never thought I'd have the strength to do. That day, love gave me a voice.

But life was not done with me yet.

The week of his funeral, one of our horses died suddenly. I had carried a nagging feeling about poisoned water, but brushed it off as paranoia. That morning, as I left for Nonno's burial, the horse was found lifeless. Two losses side by side, as if the earth itself was demanding I face endings I was not ready to face.

And then — just six weeks later — my younger brother died.

The shock was unbearable, the grief so sharp it felt surreal. Drugs had been stealing him from us slowly, but nothing prepared me for the final goodbye.

And yet, he came back.

He told me that in spirit he could do more than he ever could in this life. His words pierced my mourning, bringing comfort and clarity. He even returned with humour, playing little tricks the way he always had. Mischief was his signature, and I recognised it instantly.

Now he comes when I need him, when I doubt, when I need guidance, when I crave confirmation. Always with love.

His passing shifted something forever in me. I decided I would not let fear keep me small anymore. I would live. For me, and for him.

So I began facing my fears — skydiving, horseback archery, stepping into challenges that once paralysed me. Each bold step felt like carrying him with me, a living tribute to his spirit.

Grief broke me. But grief also became my teacher. It taught me the urgency of life, the preciousness of breath, and the courage to live fully.

Healing began slowly.

For years, people had pointed to my 'wrongness,' and there were times I did not want to be here. But I wanted to live, for my children.

I learned that emotions stored themselves in the body. Anger in the shoulders. Grief in the chest. Anxiety in the stomach. With awareness, we can release what no longer serves us. I practised breathing, scanning my body, asking, where do I feel this? I gathered the energy, honoured it, and released it.

Another friend taught me about horses and leadership. She pointed out that I walked with my eyes down, shoulders hunched — no direction, no confidence. Horses need leaders, and in that moment, I realised how far I had drifted from the child who once rode wild horses through town without fear.

I began working with Zena, a spirited quarter horse Arab. At first it was not about doing, but about breathing together, finding presence. She showed me that the challenge was not her — it was me. She asked me to listen, to trust, to be fully present.

Lady, my other quarter horse, taught me something different: to stop touching, to simply be. When she allowed me into her space, it was because I had listened.

The horses became mirrors, teaching me trust, presence, and connection. Through them, I saw how much of my life had been shaped by conditioning, expectations, and judgments that were not truly mine. I realised how often I had lived small; tethered by old stories.

Letting go was not one moment, it was a process. Each release, each breath, each connection with the horses lifted another weight. I was no longer bound by fear.

And when I let go, I realised something profound: I could fly. Not with wings, but in spirit — in freedom, in wholeness, in choosing to live fully.

Freedom starts in the body, in presence, in trusting the wisdom within. When we release what is not ours, honour our energy, and connect deeply with ourselves — the sky is not the limit. It is only the beginning. There is so much more.

So much of our life is spent believing we are at the mercy of outside circumstances — family, society, relationships, money, even fate. It is easy to feel powerless when things do not go our way. But what if that is not the full truth?

Like a tumble stone, we end up shining.

We are not our story.

What happens to us does not define who we are.

Cracks do not ruin us — they reveal us.

The lies we were told cannot contain our light.

And what if, in fact, we are the creators of our own reality?

What if we are here to learn the lessons our souls chose before we became human.

Every challenge, heartbreak, joy, or grief is part of the growth we came here to experience.

Even when the world feels unfair, your truth cannot be contained. Your inner knowing, your voice, and your choices are stronger than any system. They are the forces that shape your life. Stand in them. Honour them. Live them.

This does not mean we control every single event around us. Life still has its surprises and challenges. But we do have complete authority over how we perceive those events, what meaning we give them, and how we choose to respond. And those choices create ripple effects that shape our lives in profound ways.

Think of it this way: two people can live in the same household, experience the same event, and yet walk away with two completely different beliefs about themselves.

Why? Because each of us assigns meaning based on our own inner world. That meaning becomes a filter — a lens through which we see everything else.

Here is the exciting part: lenses can be changed. Beliefs can be rewritten. And the moment we shift our perspective, our reality shifts with it.

You have already been creating your reality — every thought you repeat, every feeling you hold onto, every story you tell yourself is a brushstroke on the canvas of your life.

The question is, are you painting a picture you love? Or are you replaying someone else's design?

A Practice for Stepping into Creation

Next time you feel stuck in a limiting belief or a heavy feeling, pause, and ask yourself:

- Does this feel light and true for me, or heavy and limiting?
- Is this thought really mine, or did I inherit it from someone else?
- If I could choose a new meaning right now, what would it be?

Notice what shifts when you ask these questions. By becoming aware, you step out of reaction and into creation. And that is where freedom begins.

Life experience is our greatest teacher. Often, it is not what we read in a book or what someone else tells us that transforms us most — it is what we live through, what we feel, and the meaning we give to those experiences.

Many people feel like they do not fit in with what society says is 'normal'. If that is you, know this: it is more than okay. You were never meant to be a carbon copy of everyone else. Each of us carries unique gifts and qualities that make us who we are.

When we base our worth on being accepted or understood by others, we risk losing our essence — our truth.

THE SOUL'S RISING

They say our basic emotional needs are love, safety, belonging, and acceptance.

When those needs are not met in childhood, we often form our own limiting beliefs.

Here is something to notice: when fear is created, people become easier to control.

Fear keeps us small. If we fear the darkness, we may look to others to guide us into the light.

But the deeper truth is this: you already hold the tools to navigate your own path.

What feels light in your body is often your inner compass pointing toward truth. What feels heavy may be a lie, an old story, or even the energy of another person that you are sensing.

Take darkness as an example. You may feel the need for protection — but from what, exactly? I clear my space and surround myself with pure love after grounding. This allows me to feel my energy clearly and prevents others from draining or taking it, not because there is any immediate danger, but so I can stay centred. If I truly feel unsafe, I can heighten that awareness so it registers as real.

Our minds are incredibly powerful. At any moment, we can shift perception; and when perception changes, so does our reality. What we focus on expands. If we focus on fear, we feed it. If we focus on possibility, we create more of it.

When I began to wake up to this, I started by asking myself questions: Does this feel light and true for me? Is it even mine; or did I inherit it from someone else? Is there a lie in the space? Is this for my highest good? These questions became the doorway into greater awareness.

Solitude helps too. When we step away from the noise of the outside world, we give ourselves the gift of stillness. In stillness, we begin to hear our own voice more clearly. We begin to remember who we are.

Awareness Break

Take a pause here. Ask yourself:
- Where in my life have I accepted a belief that doesn't feel like mine?
- What experiences shaped the story I tell myself about who I am?
- If I stopped trying to 'fit in', what part of me would feel free?
- Right now, what feels light and true for me — and what feels heavy and limiting?

Sit with your answers. You do not need to force anything. Just notice what comes. It may be a few days or instant. Allow the thoughts flow as they come and go.

"I am not what happened to me, I am what I choose to become."
— Carl Jung

Life shapes us in ways we do not control. Words, actions, and perceptions of others often define how we are seen — sometimes without our awareness. These unseen narratives leave marks on both mind and soul.

I shared a dream I had with my grandmother — a cat's unblinking gaze fixed on me, silent and unsettling. She said, "A cat in your dream is bad. It means someone is speaking ill of you behind your back." At the time, I did not understand. Later, I realised how our innocence can be mocked: kindness and trust often make us vulnerable to cruelty.

People act on what they have heard, not what they have seen. Rumours are like invisible scripts, inked by others' voices, directing how the world should see and respond to you. Psychologically, it is coercion by perception; spiritually, it's an invitation to act from truth rather than reaction. As the sayings go: "Don't believe everything you hear," and "What people say about you says more about them than you."

The loudest voices often demand attention while quieter, suffering ones go unnoticed. I became the still and calm in the eye of the cyclone, visualising myself at its centre so I could remain grounded — focused on my breath, untangling my thoughts, and reclaiming my inner world without being drawn into the chaos swirling around me.

Spiritually, solitude was sacred: a space to see how my mind had been shaped and reconnect with the self beyond borrowed narratives.

Humour, unexpectedly, became a teacher. The cat was not a warning — it was a nudge not to take whispers and gossip too seriously. "Let it roll off you like water off a duck's back" became real, though ducks do paddle madly underneath. Life taught me to float, letting the storm churn silently beneath a calm, steady surface.

Now, my personal mantra — the truth I hold above the noise — is simple and bold:

"I decide my own truth, what is real for me not the world."

Because in the end, the greatest journey is the one inward — to meet, understand, and finally love ourselves. The only truth that truly matters is the one that brings us home to ourselves.

What if the weight we carry — the echoes of our own past and the inheritance of those who came before us — forms invisible knots within us? Some call these knots demons, curses, burdens. But when we finally turn toward our emotions, we discover they were never the enemy. They were only treated as if they were dangerous, as if feeling deeply meant we were somehow flawed.

Yet our responses are simply human. Anyone placed in our story would feel something similar. The issue is not the feeling — it's that no one ever taught us how to listen to our inner world, how to walk through it with understanding instead of fear.

So, we improvise our way through life. Some are ruled by the relentless inner critic; others by impulses that silence their quieter wisdom. We are guided not by the wisest part of ourselves, but by whatever part of us learned to shout the loudest.

And when we get stuck — when we fixate, doubt, or turn against ourselves — it becomes hard to trust that the process has a direction. But it does. If we can stay with our experience instead of resisting it, something wiser, something better, eventually rises to meet us.

And this is how we rise —

not by denying the pain,

but by letting it guide us.

By allowing it to become a compass pointing toward what still needs tending.

When we choose to nurture ourselves through the process,

something softens.

We learn to offer ourselves the care we were never taught to give.

We begin to listen to the parts of us that have waited years to be heard.

And as we move with our emotions instead of against them,

we start choosing differently.

We choose what honours our greatest good,

what supports our becoming,

what allows us to grow rather than shrink.

This is not a quick ascent.

It is a slow, steady rising —

a return to ourselves,

guided by the very feelings we once feared.

Leanne Cathro

Leanne Cathro is an energy worker, mental health recovery coach, and mindfulness teacher devoted to helping others reconnect with themselves — emotionally, physically, and energetically. A wife, mother, stepmother, and grandmother, as well as an animal lover with horses and dogs, Leanne's healing path began with animals. Their honesty and sensitivity taught her how deeply energy communicates long before words do.

Today, she brings that same intuitive understanding to her work with people. Leanne teaches mindfulness techniques that gently guide individuals back into presence, grounding, and inner balance. She believes energy work is often misunderstood — not mystical, not a belief system, and certainly not a cult — but simply a compassionate way of listening to the body and caring for oneself on a deeper, more holistic level.

Her practice is grounded in the truth that healing begins with awareness, and that the smallest, most intentional rituals can create profound transformation.

⊕ www.lumeurias.com.au
❶ www.facebook.com/people/Lumeurias/100063765927299
◉ www.instagram.com/lumeurias

Scan the QR code to learn more about Leanne.

chapter 02

Remembering Who I Have Always Been

by Kerryn Slater

I came into this life awake.

I did not have language for it then, only an innate knowing that the world extended far beyond what was visible. I was highly sensitive, intuitive, and deeply aware. I could hear the thoughts of others as clearly as spoken words and feel their emotions move through my body as though they were my own. I experienced prophetic dreams, saw spirit, and spoke to God every day — not the God of doctrine or dogma, but a living, breathing presence that felt vast, intimate, and deeply personal.

At night, I felt the presence of the Divine wrap itself around me. There was a sense of being held, protected, and known. I now understand this as communion with Source consciousness, but as a child it was simply my reality. The unseen world was not separate from me; it was woven through my everyday experience.

The physical world, however, felt loud. Overstimulating. Dense. Sleep was difficult. I often lay awake at night, my nervous system buzzing with information I could not yet filter. I would hold my arm up in the darkness, staring at my hand, trying to tire myself out. One night, as I gazed into the void, my physical hand disappeared. What remained was energy — shimmering, alive, infinite. I could see it clearly. It did not frighten me. It felt familiar.

I remember wondering, with genuine frustration, why I couldn't move my hand through the wall. To me, it seemed logical that if everything was energy, then matter should be permeable. The limitations of the physical world felt unnecessary and confusing.

If I wanted to speak to one of my friends, I didn't reach for the phone. I sat quietly in front of our old dial telephone and sent messages to them with my mind. Within minutes, the phone would ring — and it would be them. To me, this was simply communication beyond form.

And yet, as natural as all of this felt internally, the world around me did not mirror my experience. I was acutely aware of my otherness. I felt different, misunderstood, and overwhelmed by the expectations of a world that did not recognise or honour sensitivity, intuition, or multidimensional awareness. I spent much of my early life confused about who I was and why I was here, carrying a deep sense of displacement — as though I had arrived without a map.

By the age of twenty-one, life delivered a profound rupture. One of my favourite aunts passed away unexpectedly, and her death shook me to my core. I felt angry with God — a word I use here because it was the language of my upbringing, though my lived experience of the Divine had always extended far beyond what I had been taught.

I questioned the meaning of life, the apparent cruelty of losing someone so young, and the randomness of suffering. I wanted answers — not platitudes or reassurances, but truth.

In the midst of this questioning, a friend invited me to a student reading day at a local Spiritualist church. Psychics in training were offering readings. I had never heard of such a thing before. The idea both terrified and intrigued me. Something in me resisted — and yet something deeper knew I needed to go.

That day changed my life.

I was stunned by the accuracy, depth, and resonance of the information shared with me. It felt as though someone had reached into the depths of my soul and spoken truths I had never articulated aloud. By the end of the reading, I was invited to attend their weekly classes.

Walking into that space for the first time, I experienced something unfamiliar and profoundly relieving: I felt normal.

For the first time in my life, I was surrounded by people who spoke the language of energy, spirit, and consciousness. I wasn't too much. I wasn't strange. I wasn't imagining things. I had found my people.

This marked the beginning of ten years of psychic mediumship development, platform work, and foundational spiritual training. It was here that I learned to work consciously with my guides, open my channel to healing energy, and trust my intuitive intelligence. My connection to spirit gave me a sense of purpose, belonging, and direction for a significant period of my life.

And yet, despite the depth of this work, I kept much of it hidden from the outside world. Beneath the surface, I unknowingly carried ancient wounds — imprints of persecution from other lifetimes where spiritual visibility had not been safe. These unconscious memories shaped my fear of being fully seen, even as I stood in my gifts.

During this time, I was also attuned as a Reiki practitioner. Working with healing energy — which I experienced as Christ consciousness — deepened my understanding of unconditional love and service. Healing was never something I did; it was something that flowed through me when I allowed myself to be an open channel. The intelligence of energy knew exactly where to go, what to soften, and what to restore.

In my early thirties, my first marriage came to an end. Making this choice required deep soul searching and came with an overwhelming sense of failure, shame, and fear. Although I knew it was the right decision for my soul, it also plunged me into depression and anxiety. I felt angry at the universe and disconnected from everything I once trusted.

For a time, I turned my back on my spiritual gifts entirely. My life swung in the opposite direction — a kind of delayed rebellion. Looking back now, I recognise this period as a spiritual crisis. Living out of alignment with my soul created anxiety, stress, self-judgment, and profound disconnection. I felt fragmented, lost, and disempowered — as though I had abandoned myself.

My reawakening came in what I can only describe as a sliding doors moment. In an instant, I saw my life flash before me. From the depths of my being, I sent an SOS out to the universe — a plea to be saved from myself. I promised that if I was given another chance, I would be of service to Source and fully embrace my spiritual path.

The universe responded — as it always does.

In late 2013, while researching something for a friend, I stumbled across an Australian organisation called Smiling Mind. It reintroduced me to meditation. I began a daily morning and evening practice, unaware that these small, consistent moments would become the doorway home to myself.

In the stillness of meditation, I felt held, seen, and heard in unconditional love. Fragmented parts of my soul began to return. I actively asked the universe to guide me, to teach me how to love, accept, and forgive myself. In the absence of judgment, a profound question arose within me: If Source knows everything about me and loves me this deeply, then surely, I must be worthy of loving myself.

During this time, while resting in the void of meditation, I began seeing two golden eyes with impossibly long lashes. They remained closed for months, yet I could feel their sacred presence. One day, completely enveloped in divine love, the eyes opened — one green, one violet. When their gaze met mine, something cracked open in my heart so powerfully it took my breath away.

In that moment, I knew — no matter who I had been, who I was, or who I was yet to become, no matter my choices or perceived failures, I was unconditionally loved. I understood then that there was nothing to forgive. Everything I had experienced had led me precisely where I needed to be.

Around this time, I experienced three life-changing visions.

The first was of being a microbiome floating peacefully in the ocean — no identity, no striving, no fear. As awareness expanded, I realised I was held within the vast consciousness of the ocean itself. The message was clear: we are never separate from the Divine; we are always held within it.

The second vision revealed the moment of conception as a cosmic event — explosive, joyful, and radiant. I heard what sounded like a symphony of angels and understood the profound impact of each soul's incarnation within the cosmos.

The third vision showed my life as a line of dominos. As each one fell, I saw how every decision, heartbreak, and choice had led me exactly here. I woke in tears, released from the weight of self-judgment. Forgiveness flowed naturally.

These experiences marked a profound rebirth. Synchronicities multiplied. Nature became my teacher. Colours intensified. Light spoke. In one meditation, I expanded beyond my body into the vastness of all that is — an experience so filled with wonder and love that returning to my physical form felt almost impossible.

This awakening ignited my calling to teach meditation. In 2014 I became a qualified meditation teacher, committed to helping others reconnect with Source and themselves.

My path continued to unfold in profound and unexpected ways through Ascension Reiki and my deepening connection with the angelic realm. Completing my attunement to Master level marked another significant initiation in my journey — one that further elevated my consciousness and attuned me to what I experienced as fifth-dimensional frequencies of love, unity, and divine intelligence.

As my nervous system and energetic body acclimatised to these higher frequencies, my perception of reality began to shift dramatically. I started to see kaleidoscopic streams of colour flowing through the rays of the sun and into my third eye, as though light itself was communicating directly with my consciousness. At times, these colours carried a language beyond words — what I came to understand as light codes, subtle transmissions of information and remembrance activating dormant aspects of my soul.

Divine messages began arriving through nature in ways that felt intimate and deeply personal. Images would form in the clouds with startling clarity, birds would appear at precise moments as messengers, and nature itself became a living oracle. I no longer felt separate from the world around me; instead, I experienced myself as part of an intelligent, responsive field of consciousness that was constantly guiding, affirming, and reflecting truth back to me.

It was during this period that the universe gently but unmistakably guided me toward spiritual teachers whose work would further anchor and refine my awakening.

Esther and Abraham Hicks' book *Ask and It Is Given* introduced me to the Law of Attraction in a way that felt expansive rather than prescriptive. Rather than focusing on control or outcome, I began to understand manifestation as a vibrational dialogue between my inner state and the universe. I started to consciously play with intention, alignment, and emotional resonance, and in doing so, I tapped into a sense of magic that had long been dormant within me.

What surprised me most was not that manifestation worked, but how deeply I had been subconsciously afraid of my own creative power. Somewhere along the way, I had absorbed the belief that desiring too much, receiving too easily, or living too joyfully was unsafe or undeserved. This work gently revealed where I had not yet felt worthy of ease, abundance, or expansion — and invited me to soften those inner constraints with compassion rather than force.

Soon after, Eckhart Tolle's *The Power of Now* entered my life and fundamentally transformed my relationship with my mind. For the first time, I truly understood that I am not my thoughts — I am the awareness observing them. This insight alone was liberating. I began to see clearly how much of my anxiety had been rooted in living in the past or projecting fear into the future, and how presence offered an immediate release from that suffering.

Through Tolle's teachings, I came to recognise the pain body within me — the accumulation of unresolved emotional pain stored in the psyche and nervous system. Rather than trying to heal or fix it, I learned to witness it with presence. In doing so, I discovered that pain dissolves not through resistance, but through conscious awareness.

Tolle's *A New Earth* deepened this awakening even further. It offered a profound exploration of the egoic self — how identity, roles, labels, superiority, inferiority, and attachment keep consciousness contracted. I began to see clearly how unconsciousness plays out collectively through power struggles, comparison, conflict, and suffering, and how a new level of human consciousness is emerging — one rooted in presence, compassion, and inner spaciousness.

I immersed myself in these teachings for over a year, not to accumulate knowledge, but to embody the wisdom. Through this process, I became acutely aware of how harshly I had treated myself throughout my life. The internal criticism, the relentless self-judgment, the belief that I needed to be better, different, or more evolved — all of it softened as I learned to observe egoic patterns without shame and allow them to loosen their grip.

This period of self-honesty and presence opened my heart in unexpected ways.

Marianne Williamson's *A Return to Love* then guided me into the teachings of *A Course in Miracles,* which became a profound catalyst for self-forgiveness and inner peace. These teachings revealed that the world we perceive through fear, judgment, and separation is an illusion created by the ego. Our true nature, beneath all conditioning, is Love — created by and eternally connected to Source.

I came to understand that suffering arises from the belief that we are separate — from God, from one another, and from love itself. Healing, then, does not occur by changing the external world, but by changing how we perceive it. This reframing was deeply liberating.

Forgiveness, as taught through *A Course in Miracles,* was unlike anything I had previously understood. It was not about condoning behaviour or denying pain, but about recognising that what I believed had harmed me was rooted in illusion — a misperception born of fear rather than truth. I learned that forgiveness releases the one who forgives, not the other, and that every grievance is ultimately a call for love.

As I practised this form of forgiveness, something profound shifted within me. Resentment softened. Emotional charge dissolved. Long-standing relational patterns healed at their root. I could see how karmic loops and repeating lessons had been sustained not by circumstance, but by perception — and how forgiveness gently untangled them.

Forgiveness became the key that unlocked peace.

This phase of my journey was not about bypassing pain or striving for spiritual perfection. It was about coming home to myself with honesty, humility, and love. It taught me that awakening is not an ascent away from our humanity, but a deepening into it — where presence, compassion, and truth can finally take root.

By early 2014, I had transformed my language, my consciousness, and my relationship with the Divine.

I began my business, offering healings, readings, and meditation classes — not as someone who had it all figured out, but as a woman who had walked the path of remembering and was now being asked to walk alongside others.

I stepped into the role of teacher, sharing the wisdom, knowledge, and lived experiences that had shaped my awakening, with the intention of supporting others in their own journeys of self-discovery and spiritual awakening. In doing so, my seeking softened into service, and my devotion to truth, expansion, and self-remembering deepened through guiding others back to themselves.

Since 2020, my work — and my inner life — has continued to evolve in ways that feel deeply aligned with the unfolding of my own consciousness. My desire to more deeply understand who I am, my purpose in this lifetime, and my connection to intuition and Source consciousness has remained at the forefront of my daily life. This commitment is not abstract or occasional; it is something I live and breathe. I continue to prioritise my own personal and spiritual growth so that I may lead by example — not from perfection, but from presence, integrity, and lived experience.

What once began as a personal journey of awakening has matured into an embodied path of service, where insight becomes integration and wisdom becomes something that can be shared in practical, compassionate ways.

~

I was introduced to the Thrive Factor Archetype Framework®, which offered one of the most transformative mirrors I had encountered. Through the lens of my unique Archetypes, I gained deeper insight into the patterns, strengths, and challenges that have shaped my life. Rather than pathologising my sensitivity and depth, this framework honoured them as intrinsic aspects of who I am.

This insight reignited my passion to support women in understanding themselves beyond conditioning, roles, and expectations. It felt like a natural evolution of my work, and I went on to become a Licensed Thrive Factor Coach®, integrating this framework into my self-discovery coaching so women could reconnect with their authentic strengths and innate wisdom.

Around the same time, I became a ThetaHealing® practitioner, a modality that deepened my capacity for inner work and transformation. By working directly with the subconscious mind, ThetaHealing® allowed both my clients and me to identify and gently release the hidden beliefs that shape our lives, supporting ongoing growth, healing, and evolution.

~

It was during this period that I remember saying to the universe, half in jest, "I really hope my next uplevelling isn't through grief." Even as the words left my lips, I felt a tremor of uncertainty — was this intuitive knowing, or simply fear of losing those I loved?

In the years that followed, I lost two beloved pets whose passing broke my heart. And then came the deepest loss of all — the death of my father, followed by the passing of my mother just four months later. Their deaths left me utterly unanchored. The ground beneath me disappeared, and I knew instinctively that this was not a time for spiritual bypassing or platitudes.

I understood, at a soul level, that I would need to meet this grief fully. I would need to allow space for the heartache, the anger, the confusion, and the depth of the loss to move through me. This period brought to the surface unresolved beliefs and wounds I did not even realise were still living within me.

The last few years, I sought professional support while also continuing my development as a Theta Healing® practitioner. I believe it was the combination of these grounded supports, my unwavering connection to Source, and my ongoing connection with my parents in spirit that carried me through.

I'll be honest — this was one of the most difficult periods of my life. A true dark night of the soul. It called for surrender. It called for trust, radical acceptance, and deep self-compassion. Most of all, it called for honesty. I did not shy away from the inner work. I brought everything to the surface — no matter how uncomfortable or vulnerable it felt — and allowed it to be seen, felt, and healed.

In time, I began to recognise the quiet alchemy taking place beneath the grief. My connection to the all-that-is deepened. My intuition expanded even further. Trust in myself, my gifts, and who I am solidified in ways I had never known before. My relationship with the Divine became more grounded, embodied, and real — not something I reached for in moments of transcendence, but something I lived in daily communion with.

What has emerged from this season was not a return to who I was before, but a deeper embodiment of who I truly am. Wiser. Softer. Stronger. And more anchored in truth than ever before.

I am deeply grateful for every soul who has walked beside me — those who supported me, those who challenged me, and even those whose presence brought pain. Each experience has shaped my awakening, refining my compassion, resilience, and truth. Through it all, the presence of the Divine has never left me. In my darkest moments, it did not remove me from my humanity, but gently guided me back into it with love, placing the right teachers, experiences, and reminders in my path exactly when I was ready to receive them.

Closing Reflection: Souls Rising

Awakening, I have learned, is not a single moment of illumination. It is a remembering — sometimes gentle, sometimes fierce — of who we are beneath layers of conditioning and fear.

There have been moments on my path when awakening felt expansive and filled with light, and others when it felt like a descent into shadow and unravelling. Both have been sacred. Both have been initiations.

True awakening does not remove us from our humanity; it brings us more fully into it. It teaches us to meet discomfort with presence, to hold our shadows with compassion rather than judgment, and to remember that we are not here to be fixed, but to be loved.

The rising of souls unfolding now is quiet and intimate. It happens in moments of stillness, in the courage it takes to live truthfully, and in the choice to dissolve old identities and return to authenticity.

My relationship with the Divine has been a lifelong dialogue. Even when I forgot myself, it never forgot me.

If there is one truth I offer, it is this:

Your path does not need to mirror another's.

Your sensitivity is not a weakness — it is wisdom.

You are never separate.

You are always held.

And remembering who you are is the most sacred journey of all.

Kerryn Slater

Kerryn Slater is a Spiritual Alchemist, women's self-discovery coach, and intuitive guide with over three decades of experience in psychic mediumship, energy healing, and spiritual development. She is the founder of Holistic Essentials where she supports women to heal, awaken, and reconnect with their innate wisdom through meditation, intuitive guidance, archetypal coaching, and energy healing.

Kerryn is a certified Meditation Teacher, Reiki Master Teacher (specialising in Ascension/Angelic Reiki), ThetaHealing® practitioner, and Licensed Thrive Factor Coach®. She is the creator of the Divine Goddess Oracle Deck and co-hosts international retreats for women ready to reclaim their voice, worth, and inner knowing.

Her work bridges ancient spiritual wisdom with grounded transformational tools, offering a compassionate and embodied approach to awakening.

Kerryn lives in Australia and continues to walk the path of remembrance alongside the women she serves.

⊕ www.holisticessentials.com.au
❶ www.facebook.com/HolisticEssentialsTherapyandConsulting
◎ www.instagram.com/kerryn_holisticessentials_

Scan the QR code to learn more about Kerryn.

chapter 03

From the Dust Comes Beauty
by Linda Usope

From the Dust Comes Beauty

My story begins like any other child who believes in what they see and hear as real. I had been seeing spirits — or what I was told were ghosts — since I could remember. As a small child, I knew no different. I had no one to tell me it was not normal, or at least not as normal as society would have me believe. My make-believe friends were real, existing in a world so different to their siblings' experience. My mother told me I had a vivid imagination and that maybe I'd write a book someday.

Always feeling different, trying to run away from a young age without knowing why, like I didn't quite fit into this world. Outside, in nature, was my safe place. Seeing things that scared me was not easy.

In a child's mind, brought up with religion, I was visited by what I thought were monsters — people with horrible injuries. My mind went to zombies. How do you process that when no one believes that's what you see?

My father, whom I adored, left us when I was young and passed before he made 30. I never had the opportunity to say goodbye. When my dad passed, his family disconnected us in so many ways, but my Nan — my dad's mum — stayed close to us and kept my dad alive, as we were not allowed to talk about him growing up. My world was so confusing.

My mother remarried to a man with four children. I had three birth siblings as well, so eight kids, two adults in a four-bed, one-bathroom home. My life changed again dramatically. There were good times but most of all sad. I almost lost my mum twice to illness. My mum's mum — my beautiful Nan, whom I adored — helped me through so many tough times, believed in me and loved me unconditionally. I miss her so much. When she passed, I lost a part of me.

But I guess in hindsight, I got to know my dad more in death as he visited me often and my Nan has always been there when I needed her the most. I could not complain they passed, as I still see them and they have always been there to watch over my mum, as she is an incredible survivor.

Through all those tough years, I left home at 19 and started to rely on me. This is what I believed now, after many years of hard lessons that needed to be learnt. Constantly being told, "It's all in your head, you're making things up," I knew people who passed before anyone else did. I just knew things before they happened.

Life was never easy. I was told I was an attention seeker amongst many other things. I had step-siblings who I wanted to believe cared, and growing up I felt they did. But I had rose-coloured glasses on back then and had a stepfather who wished I didn't exist, which made what I was and what I saw even more difficult. Always what I recall, the black sheep in the family.

Funny thing is, many years later, he became a good grandfather to most of my children, and I helped care for him with Mum and took him to so many appointments through his illness as he went blind and was grateful. He asked me to forgive him for things that happened. I accepted and thanked him for being a good grandfather to my children.

Funny how things can turn around, but it's about learning and letting go of things that you cannot control, learning that forgiveness is a sense of letting go and understanding what I can take from this and what did I learn.

The hardest thing at that time was losing my stepbrother (whom I adored). He passed away, and then just six weeks later, my stepfather passed as well.

During that period of sadness, my family came together to grieve. We have different lives and have gone separate ways, but my brother in death brought us all together one last time. Truly blessed. I know now I chose this family, this life, this is why I am who I am. Being born empathetic sometimes is hard as we put so much energy into being there for everyone, no matter what life gives us.

I have had two really bad relationships with physical and mental abuse in both, but I was blessed with three amazing children who chose me to be their mum. Out of the dust comes beauty, but there were more lessons to learn. I had been told, "You're crazy, bipolar, you need help, you're abusive, you're not a good parent. No one will look at a crazy woman." But that taught me to be independent, to teach my children their worthiness and to believe in life, and to stand up for who I am and what I believe. I am different and that's okay.

I needed to find myself and own who I am to get it right.

I finally found someone who believed in me — my soulmate, my husband. Might I say, when I first met him he was sceptical of my gifts, but he believed in me as a person. It's not easy dating someone who talks to people no one else can see, but that did not scare him off. He helped me to grow. We have been together now for over 34 years, married with another beautiful child.

I had to connect back to myself, putting the broken pieces back together. And when I got it, I got that 'OMG' moment where I knew everything I see, hear, feel, know is real and I'm not the only one who communicates with people crossed over.

I finally had someone who held space for me to be me and wouldn't let go no matter how crazy this life I was living — he was up for the ride. I could finally take the fear out of what I see. I could talk to whoever I wanted, dead or living.

I took the Hollywood out of what I perceived was real and what was not, understanding everyone needs to be heard, living or not. Media has a lot to answer for when it comes to distorting truth and selling good films, creating what we all tend to believe is real.

This changed my life, my perspective, my truth. I know half my life was hard lessons that I had to live, to experience all the universe had to throw at me and understand why. I have so much to be grateful for and learning to finally connect to my truth, to self, to spirit.

So we never forget lessons but embrace them for what they are. Forgiveness will always set you free, as I strongly believe I wrote my story, my life before I got here with the help of my spiritual guides, my team.

THE SOUL'S RISING

I was born of service with love, compassion and empathy. It was all in divine timing. When the time was right to share my story, as my mentor once said, "Own it Linda. Connections with spirit only come with love. They chose you, you chose to be here to help and they will help you to help many every step of the way." So believe we are here and now we work together with love.

We are all born with amazing intuition. Some of us have been chosen to take it further. First, you have to surrender to spirit, listen. There is so much that needs to be heard, seen and felt.

I know I'm not crazy, but blessed to be of service, to be helping so many souls crossed over, talking to dead people, helping to heal souls, animals, our land, our universe. But my journey has taken me so much further than I could ever have believed.

I am happily married and now have four amazing, confident, intuitive children who can believe in everything they see and know, allowing them to be true to what they see and feel. I have five incredible grandchildren and I also know there's more to come — two beautiful little great-grandchildren. I feel another one very close. All of them are okay and proud of their mum and Nan, as I am of them. Their intuition is above and beyond. I am so blessed they are in this world at this time.

As for me growing up, I was not believed. I was called a witch, I was called crazy. I can now walk down the street, holding the phone against my ear and talk to the living or dead and no one thinks I'm crazy.

I have travelled and continue to travel the world with my work and have fine-tuned my teaching with an incredible teacher in America, my mentor Lisa Williams. She teaches in a little town outside of Buffalo called Lily Dale, where modern day spiritualism began, where people could talk to spirit and not get arrested. Women finally had a voice. This is where the Fox sisters first connected, where the tapping from spirit was recorded and witnessed by so many.

Lisa, might I say, kicked my butt and allowed me to believe I was good enough and was chosen to do this work. Her words to me were, "Linda, it's time to believe in who you are and own your shit."

I wasn't sure if I'm her mother or she's mine in a past life, but I'll tell you, we are soul connected and I knew from the first time I saw her, it was not what she wore or what she looked like. It was about her connection and trust, delivering messages of hope and love. We were connected instantly.

I will always be grateful for her and her belief in me. She is one of many teachers and mentors who came into my life. I have had the privilege to be connected and trained by some of the most incredible teachers and mentors around the world whose paths I'm blessed to have crossed and I'm sure there will be many more whose paths I will cross, as we are always learning and evolving.

And for all the students over the many years I've helped, being a small part of their journey as they have honoured and trusted me along the way, has been a privilege. As I have always said, a teacher is someone who can help fine-tune your own abilities and most of all believe in you, but we cannot make you. Spirit teaches us everyday, and we are all unique, we are all put together for reasons, no coincidence.

One of my biggest lessons, or shall I say places and things I have done, is all the jobs that I have engaged in over the years. I was a checkout chick, worked for the Department of Social Security, black and white catering, bar work, aged care work, holding hands to those that were close to coming home, watching that beautiful transition from this world to the spirit world, watching who's waiting. Understanding no one dies alone, so blessed. Teacher's aid, helping kids believe in themselves, cell support for young offenders, police station as well as many volunteer jobs, which was so rewarding. So many roles of service which also helped me put bread and butter on my table and help me raise my children.

As I said earlier, I'm of service. My proudest is being a mum to four beautiful children who chose me. They will always be my blessing, my world.

Today being of service to spirit and what I do now, I am forever blessed. I cannot tell you enough how comforting and complete I am. My honour is to spirit, my work. I am blessed to have four incredible grown-up, intelligent, independent, caring children, always there for others, all of service in one way or another.

I travel to so many beautiful countries today — England, America, Egypt, New Zealand — teaching, touring, doing shows and teaching on cruise ships, travelling all around Australia, sharing my knowledge and connecting to so many, helping and watching my students grow and believe in themselves and their own abilities.

When I was little I had no one to teach me or understand what I was seeing. It's no one's fault. It was a different time.

Religion played a big part in our country back then. I guess I stayed in the church right up to my 20s. I thought prayer would make it stop, but it only kept it at bay.

As I know now, I always had control. I live with what I see. I'm not crazy. I am so blessed in so many ways unimaginable. I just needed someone to show me how. I still have an incredible amount of faith, but it's spiritual faith now. I believe in the teachings of many and the lessons we learn along the way.

I have an amazing space in Campbelltown, NSW, where I connect to so many through teaching, running classes, demonstrations (platform readings) and meditation.

I found meditation keeps me grounded and connected to self, but it can also take me to places. My guides, extended masters, angels and my creator teach me the things I need to know, whether it's a warning, premonition or helping me. They are my team, my tribe.

My main guide is the one who came down with me the moment I took my first breath. And when the time comes to take me Home, I call him my bouncer at my door. He helps me and guides me in situations that I can't always see as a human. After all we are spiritual beings living a human existence and we always have lessons to learn. It's our way of learning and evolving. He is my best friend.

I can rely on the guidance, listening to that inner voice. Sometimes, as all females do, we over-analyse things; but if you hear it, you get it and not overthink it — it will always be the truth.

I know I am here to help those believe in the spirit world, to help those who have lost loved ones believe we never really die. Our soul is eternal, our body leaves us, our loved ones are with us always. Life as we know it changes and we grieve for the ones we lose, but they're okay. And the spirit world is excited as you are welcomed home, free of all ailments that kept you trapped in the human body that was not working anymore. But their love, their connection to their loved one stays connected, and that is beautiful knowledge to me, to help them connect to family, loved ones, fur babies. They are all love and eternal.

I had the opportunity many years ago to work in a police station. I worked there for 10 years, loved it and the people I connected to. I had been reading for many police officers over my time there, working as well as them picking my brain. At first it was just a novelty to so many, but through my time and them getting to know me, I feel I had a beautiful connection with so many.

Don't get me wrong, not everyone is a believer. How do I get my information, if I'm not a detective, and that's taken the ego out of you. It's not about you, it's about your truth, giving them what you get, walking away knowing you have delivered your truth and they can put the pieces together and not taking the hard work they do on a daily basis. It's about non-judgments.

I have seen so much and been blessed to be with such incredible people of service with unbelievable intuition who did not even know where their gut instinct came from.

But so many questioned me. I became close friends with so many who I still hold dear to my heart today. One special friend I had coffee with every morning worked in forensics as an evidence officer. I was training in evidence in my work and it just gelled together. This is what I should be doing, right place, right time, coincidence? I don't think so.

So now I help with law enforcement in different ways, as well as families of crime victims and cold cases. We are of service and our knowledge should be shared to help them see things through different eyes. I'm so blessed for the work and opportunities to be a part of the process, helping those who put in the hard work with evidence collected.

My journey has been long, but I believe it has only just begun — my dedication to spirit, my work with love, empathy and compassion continues on. I have no regrets with life, just gratitude, and I thank everyone who has come and gone in my life.

Without my lessons, I believe my life would have been very different. I would have had to go through so much to feel it, to work for those who need me, and to understand that everyone has a journey on this earthly plane.

But this is just the beginning, not the end, endless blessings and love.

Trust and surrender, you are good enough, Linda xxx

Linda Usope

Linda Usope is an International Psychic Medium, Master Teacher with LWISSD (Lisa Williams International School of Spiritual Development), and a full-time spiritual practitioner.

Gifted from early childhood, Linda's life path led her through extensive service roles including nursing, aged care, schools, police support, youth offender services, and family advocacy. These experiences refined her intuition and deepened her dedication to Spirit.

She trained internationally with some of the world's leading psychic mediums and completed her Master Teacher studies in Lily Dale, New York, one of the most respected spiritual communities globally. Her work has taken her across Egypt, the USA, UK, New Zealand, the Pacific Islands, and throughout Australia, demonstrating and teaching mediumship worldwide.

Linda is a Psychic Medium, Meditation Instructor, Reiki Master, Hypnotherapist, and Matrix Timeline Therapy practitioner. She teaches psychic and medium development from beginner to advanced, including forensic mediumship, mentoring, workshops, retreats, and one-on-one training.

⊕ https://lindausope.setmore.com
❶ www.facebook.com/linda.usope
◉ www.instagram.com/lindausope

Scan the QR code to learn more about Linda.

chapter 04

The Woman Who Walks Between Worlds
by Jo Rolfe

The Woman Who Walks Between Worlds

My hands were shaking as I placed them on my daughter's body. Tayla lay on the couch, fourteen years old, pale as death, her skin clammy and cold. She had been violently ill since the surgery that morning — all four wisdom teeth removed. What should have been routine had turned into something else entirely. Her body was rejecting everything. The painkillers. The water. Even the air seemed too much for her. She shook beneath my palms, her small frame trembling with waves of nausea that wouldn't stop. Every few minutes, she would lurch forward, dry heaving, tears streaming down her face. I could see the fear in her eyes. The confusion. The silent question: What's wrong with me?

I didn't have an answer. Not one that made logical sense. But I had something else.

I closed my eyes and felt the familiar presence gather around me. The air in the room shifted, grew warmer, denser. My Spirit team — the shadows I had known since childhood, the whispers I had trusted my entire life — moved closer. I could feel them as clearly as I felt my daughter's heartbeat beneath my hands. I didn't think about what to do. I didn't question whether it would work. I simply knew.

With a voice that came from somewhere deeper than my throat, I commanded the illness to leave her body.

The room held its breath.

And then Tayla began to vomit. Not the dry heaving from before, but deep, purging waves that seemed to come from her very core. I held her hair back, whispering reassurances, feeling the energy moving through her — clearing, releasing, expelling whatever darkness had taken hold. Minutes passed. The vomiting slowed. Stopped.

She looked up at me, her eyes clearer than they had been all day. The colour was returning to her cheeks. The trembling had ceased.

"Take me home," she said quietly.

We were already on our way to the doctor's office, but something had shifted. By the time we arrived, she was sitting upright in the car, no longer clutching her stomach, no longer pale with pain. The doctor examined her, found nothing alarming, and sent us home with instructions to rest.

In the car on the way back, I gripped the steering wheel and let the truth wash over me.

I was a healer. Not in theory. Not in hope. Not in wishful thinking. My gifts were real. And I had just saved my daughter's life.

I had always known I was different.

Even as a child in Christchurch, New Zealand, I felt things others didn't feel. I saw things others didn't see. I sensed presence in empty rooms, heard whispers that weren't imagined, felt the air shift when spirits moved near.

I remember my first earthquake and the sixth sense that rose in me before anything happened. Something in the air didn't feel right. I was four years old at kindy — what we now call daycare — and one moment I was playing, the next my whole body went still. A knowing washed over me, ancient and absolute.

Without thinking, I climbed under my desk and yelled, "The earth is going to move! The earth is going to move!"

Seconds later, the rumbling began.

The teachers panicked, shouting for everyone to get under their desks. Fear erupted in the room like a second quake. I felt all of it — my own terror, the terror of the children around me, the frantic energy of the adults who didn't know what to do. It hit me like a tidal wave, overwhelming and suffocating.

So, I did the only thing that felt natural. I took big, deep breaths. I started chanting — words I didn't understand but somehow remembered. Then came the phrase that poured out of me like instinct: "I love you, I love you, I love you."

And then I saw it. A white shining light — huge, bright, radiant —

filling the space around me. It wasn't imagination. It wasn't fear. It was a presence. Protection. A force so powerful and familiar that my tiny body relaxed instantly.

Around the white light, a soft blue glow began to shimmer and dance, moving like waves of energy wrapping around us. The blue light felt strong, steady, protective — like a shield forming in the chaos. I didn't know the meaning then, but I know it now. Blue is the colour of Archangel Michael. The angel of protection. The guardian who steps forward when fear rises.

In that moment, I knew we were safe. I knew we were being held. I knew I wasn't alone.

Archangel Michael was with me that day. And he has been with me ever since.

That moment didn't awaken my gifts — it confirmed them. It showed me that the unseen wasn't something to fear. It was something that had always been guiding me, protecting me, preparing me for the life I was destined to live.

When my parents moved us to Australia, something cracked open inside me. I was still young, but I felt the shift in my bones. The land recognised me. The energy wrapped around me like a welcome I didn't yet understand. Australia didn't just become home — it felt like the place my soul had always belonged.

The air tasted different here. Softer. Freer. The sky stretched wider than anything I had ever seen, as if it was inviting me to expand with it. The ocean carried a rhythm that matched my heartbeat, and the bush behind our home became my sanctuary. I would slip away with my blanket, settle into the earth, and let the sounds of birds, insects, and rustling leaves wash over me. It was the first place I learned to listen — not with my ears, but with my whole being.

The land spoke in ways I didn't have language for yet. It soothed the ache of abandonment. It steadied the fear of the unknown. It whispered that I was held, guided, and never truly alone.

Then, my beloved father left our family.

THE SOUL'S RISING

He said goodbye to me while I was sitting in a bathtub. That was the moment everything split. I didn't understand the words he was saying, but I understood the finality in his voice. We had been in Australia for less than six months — new country, new rules, new everything — and suddenly my father was standing over me, telling me he was leaving my mother and our family. I remember staring up at him, water cooling around my small body, unable to make sense of how a goodbye could happen in a place meant for safety.

My father was ex-army. Disciplined. Structured. A man who lived by routine and duty. My mother ran the home with the same quiet strength, holding everything together while he was away for work or sports. That was our normal. Dad gone, Dad home, Dad gone again. I grew up in the rhythm of absence and return.

Some of my earliest memories are of driving to Invercargill with pure excitement, bouncing in the back seat as we went to collect him. The way my heart would race when I saw him walking toward us, uniform crisp, smile wide. That was my daddy. The hero. The man who lifted me high into the air and made me feel like the world was safe.

And yet, this was the same man who abandoned his family less than six months after bringing us across the world. No family. No friends. No support network. My mother was suddenly alone in a foreign country with children to raise and no one to lean on. Everything had changed. The ground beneath us had shifted, and I learned far too young that safety could disappear without warning.

But even in the chaos, something ancient inside me stayed awake.

Just up the road from our newly purchased home stood a small local church. Nothing grand. Nothing ornate. But the music called to me.

At seven years old, I would sneak out and slip into the pews, drawn by a presence I couldn't explain. I didn't understand doctrine or theology, but I understood energy. I understood Spirit. I understood the way the air changed when people gathered with open hearts.

I remember the sunlight streaming through the windows, catching dust particles that danced like tiny spirits in the air. I remember the music vibrating through my chest, awakening something that felt older than my body. I remember the way my skin tingled when people prayed — not because of the words, but because of the intention behind them. The sincerity. The surrender. The opening.

One Sunday, my mother found me there and dragged me out, terrified by what she didn't understand. But I wasn't afraid. I felt peace there. Belonging. Connection. I felt seen in a way I didn't feel anywhere else.

That was the beginning of my lifelong relationship with the unseen — a relationship that would guide me, challenge me, break me open, and eventually lead me to build one of the Sunshine Coast's most transformative healing studios.

But before any of that could happen, I had to survive what came next.

My marriage ended because of domestic violence.

I don't share this lightly, but I share it because it matters. Because so many women carry shame around what was never theirs to carry. Because silence protects the wrong people.

For years, I thought the violence was a reflection of my worth. In reality, it was a reflection of his wounds, his choices, and his refusal to take responsibility for his own pain.

Domestic violence doesn't always begin with bruises. It begins with subtle shifts — control disguised as concern, criticism disguised as guidance, isolation disguised as love. It begins with you slowly losing pieces of yourself until one day you look in the mirror and don't recognise the woman staring back.

I became a version of myself I didn't know how to save. I was exhausted, hyper-vigilant, and constantly trying to anticipate the next storm. I was raising children while trying to survive a man who was supposed to love me.

Leaving took more strength than staying ever did. People misunderstand that. Staying is what you do when you're trying to keep your family together, when you're hoping things will change, when you're still believing the apologies and the promises. Leaving requires a different kind of courage — the courage to choose uncertainty over familiar pain, the courage to rebuild from nothing, the courage to protect your children even when your heart is breaking.

I walked away not just for myself, but for my children. For their future. For their sense of safety. For the generational patterns I refused to pass down. I walked away because I finally understood that love should not hurt, that partnership should not diminish you, and that my children deserved to see their mother rise, not disappear.

But leaving didn't instantly heal the patterns that shaped me. Survival mode doesn't switch off just because the relationship ends. Trauma doesn't evaporate the moment you walk out the door. I was free, but I was also carrying years of conditioning — beliefs about myself, my worth, and what I thought I deserved. Those beliefs followed me into the next chapter of my life.

My second long-term relationship came after the marriage, and it unfolded quickly. I fell pregnant six months in, giving me my third child, a son. At the time, I told myself this was a fresh start, a chance to build something different from what I had survived. On the surface, it did look different. There was no physical violence, no shouting, no explosive moments that left me bracing for impact. Because of that, I convinced myself it was healthier. I wanted so badly to believe I had finally chosen better.

But emotional unavailability can be its own kind of wound. Silence can bruise just as deeply as words. Distance can feel like abandonment in slow motion. There were no fists, but there was a constant absence — an absence of presence, of partnership, of emotional safety. I was raising a baby with a man who thought that giving me a credit card was the solution to every problem. As if financial provision could replace connection. As if money could substitute for love, support, or accountability. As if I should be grateful enough to ignore the quiet ache in my chest telling me I was repeating a cycle I desperately wanted to break.

What I didn't understand then was that I was still operating from survival. I had left violence, but I hadn't yet healed the beliefs that kept me choosing emotionally unavailable men. I didn't recognise the red flags because they felt familiar — familiarity masquerading as comfort. When you grow up or live long enough in chaos, calm can feel suspicious, and emotional distance can feel normal.

I stayed longer than I should have, not because I didn't know something was wrong, but because I didn't yet believe I deserved better. I told myself it was "good enough". I told myself I could make it work. I told myself that having both parents under one roof mattered more than the quiet erosion of my spirit.

But a home without emotional safety is not a home. It is a holding pattern. A place where you shrink yourself to keep the peace. A place where your needs become negotiable. A place where you learn to carry the weight of the relationship alone because asking for more feels dangerous, or pointless, or both.

There were moments when I tried to speak my truth, to express what I needed, to ask for partnership instead of performance. But every conversation circled back to the same message: here's the card, here's the money, here's the solution. As if my heart could be bought. As if my loneliness could be fixed with transactions.

This relationship became another mirror — one I didn't want but desperately needed. It reflected back the parts of me still waiting to be healed: the part that equated stability with settling, the part that believed love required self-abandonment, the part that thought survival was the same as happiness. And in that reflection, I began to see the woman I was slowly becoming. A woman who was learning to listen to her intuition. A woman who was beginning to understand her worth. A woman who was no longer willing to repeat the same story.

And in the thirteen years that followed, I raised my children alone.

THE SOUL'S RISING

Those years were a crucible. A forging. A transformation. I learned how to stretch a dollar, how to hold my children through their fears, how to rebuild a life from the ground up. I learned how to be mother, father, provider, protector, and nurturer all at once.

My focus was survival, stability, and love.

But this is also the part of my story where I turned on myself. Where I shut my gifts down. Where I numbed the very intuition that had always guided me.

I worked as a senior manager with thirty staff, holding everything together on the outside while falling apart on the inside. Every night I drank — one bottle of wine, then two — anything to quiet the noise in my body. Anything to silence the truth I wasn't ready to face.

Yes, the candles still burned in our home. Yes, the essential oils still filled the air. Yes, Spirit still wandered through the rooms, offering guidance, whispering reminders, refusing to leave until I ushered them into the light.

But I wasn't listening. I didn't want to listen.

My daughter's best friend — gone too soon at just sixteen — visited me constantly. She changed my morning music. She sent signs day and night. She nudged, guided, comforted, and still I poured another glass. And another. And another.

I went to more churches, searching for myself in every sermon, every song, every altar call. I was desperate to feel something other than the ache inside me. Desperate to remember who I was beneath the exhaustion, the responsibility, the grief, the wine.

This wasn't healing. This was survival. This was me trying to outrun the very gifts that would one day save me.

And yet, even in my darkest, most disconnected years, Spirit never left. My gifts never left. They simply waited for the moment I was ready to return to myself.

And then came Tayla's surgery. The moment that changed everything.

After that day, I couldn't ignore it anymore. My daughter's recovery was too fast, too complete, too undeniable. What I had done with my hands, my voice, my intention — it was real. It had always been real.

I began to explore my gifts more deeply.

As my children grew older, my spiritual abilities expanded in ways I could no longer deny. My daughter's best friends died by suicide and grief entered our home like a storm. But with the grief came signs. Messages. Presence. They changed her music. They sent her songs. They whispered through energy. They knew I could hear them.

More shadows appeared each time someone left this earth. Then my step-sister passed — and wouldn't leave my home. She lingered, confused, stuck between worlds. I felt her. Saw her. Heard her. And with love and certainty, I guided her to the light.

That was the moment I realised the truth: I was a channel for spirits who were stuck between worlds.

This wasn't imagination. This wasn't a coincidence. This was my calling.

I began to understand that death was not an ending — it was a transition. A doorway. A shift in frequency. And I was someone who could hear the echoes of the in-between.

In my early twenties, tarot cards had entered my life. What began as curiosity amongst friends quickly became a powerful tool for channelling Spirit. I would sit at kitchen tables, cards spread before me, and feel messages flow through me with startling clarity. The more I listened, the stronger my psychic mediumship became. I learned to trust the first message that came through. I learned to speak what I heard, even when it made no sense to me. I learned that Spirit never lies.

Thirty years later, my readings are known across Australia for their accuracy, depth, and truth. Clients don't call them readings — they call them 'tellings'. Because I don't predict. I reveal. I activate. I tell the truth your soul already knows.

THE SOUL'S RISING

As my children stepped into adulthood, I finally had the space to deepen into the path that had been calling me since childhood. I dedicated myself to learning, training, and mastering the modalities that would shape my life's work.

I became a Reiki Master, a Sacred Cacao Facilitator Trainer, an Access Bars Facilitator Trainer, a Menopause and Perimenopause Coach, a Somatics Facilitator, a Munay-Ki and Womb Rites Facilitator, and a Life and Business Coach.

Every modality expanded me. Every training sharpened me. Every initiation awakened another layer of my purpose. I wasn't collecting certificates. I was remembering who I had always been.

I began to understand that my life had never been random. Every hardship was an initiation. Every challenge was a lesson. Every moment of survival was preparing me to guide others through their own darkness.

With decades of experience, mastery, and spiritual authority behind me, I birthed something extraordinary: The Spiritual Vibe Holistic Healing Studio in Birtinya, Queensland.

A sanctuary. A safe and beautiful place to heal. A space where people come home to themselves.

The studio is more than a business — it is a living extension of my soul. A place where Spirit moves freely. A place where healing is not just offered, but embodied. A place where people feel seen, held, and transformed.

Clients walk in carrying the weight of their lives. They walk out remembering who they are.

I built the studio with intention in every corner. The colours. The textures. The scents. The energy. Everything was chosen to support healing, awakening, and remembrance.

People don't just visit my studio. They experience it.

Today, I am one of the Sunshine Coast's most sought-after healers, intuitive readers, and spiritual mentors. My work reaches far beyond my studio — through online readings, courses, training, and the countless lives I touch every day.

I am a mother. A healer. A medium. A shaman. A coach. A guide. A woman who walks confidently between worlds.

When I think back to that afternoon with Tayla — her shaking body beneath my hands, the moment I commanded the illness to leave, the wave of knowing that washed over me — I understand now that it wasn't the beginning.

It was the remembering.

I had always been this. I had always carried this gift. Life had simply been preparing me, testing me, refining me until I was ready to step fully into my power.

My story is not just a story of spiritual gifts. It is a story of resilience. Of awakening. Of purpose. Of a woman who turned her pain into power, her intuition into mastery, and her life into medicine.

And I am only just beginning.

 ## *Jo Rolfe*

As the Conscious Life Creator at The Spiritual Vibe Holistic Healing Studio in Birtinya, Jo brings a fierce devotion to awakening, embodiment, and radical self-remembrance. Her work is forged through lived experience — every initiation, every rebirth, every moment of truth fuels the way she guides others into their own power. Jo weaves intuitive, energetic, and somatic modalities to ignite clarity, courage, and conscious creation in those ready to rise.

The Spiritual Vibe is more than a studio. It is a home to reset, reclaim balance, and return to the fire of your own inner knowing. Within this sanctuary, Jo holds space for deep transformation, emotional alchemy, spiritual expansion, and the reclamation of your authentic voice.

Jo's mission is to activate the collective — one awakening at a time — by reminding humanity what becomes possible when we choose to live consciously, boldly, and unapologetically aligned with our soul's truth.

🌐 www.thespiritualvibehealingstudio.com.au
❶ www.facebook.com/thespiritualvibe111
◉ www.instagram.com/thespiritualvibe111
Scan the QR code to learn more about Jo.

chapter 05

Awakening From My Deep Slumber
by Korinna Zoya Hunter

The term 'awakening' is elusive. Let me explain it in a creative way.

Imagine a plant with a million eyes in the form of buds. Each bud is waiting to be activated, awakened. One bud gets activated, the eye opens, switching itself on, revealing its light. After some time, it dims again. That street light is no longer accessible to you. You go back to your normal slumber state.

Later, you activate that same bud; its eye opens again, but this time a little stronger. The buds next to it also begin to activate and open as new links and street lights are revealed. You have created new neural pathways. New, unexplored roads light up before you. This gives you moments of heightened awareness, new possibilities, and creative solutions, tapping more into your unlimited potential self. If you use these new neural pathways enough times, they strengthen. This makes it easier to maintain this new state of awareness and apply it every day.

No one is 'higher' than another. We are all opening up different layers of awareness that are right for us, depending on where we are on our spiritual journey. Some souls are very new, and others have been around since the beginning of creation.

But here, I am going to talk about my own personal journey.

Firstly, I was not your typical child. I did not fit in, no matter how hard I tried. I felt like a total stranger, that I didn't belong anywhere. I was a big dreamer and a highly sensitive child longing for support and love to navigate my life and true path. My support did not come from expected sources — not through my family or other human beings.

I found solitude among nature: climbing the carob tree in my grandmother's yard, playing with beetles and chameleons, or picking wild poppy flowers in the open field. I did not feel safe around humans. I kept holding on to hope that a better life was ahead of me — hope that I would be loved and accepted.

THE SOUL'S RISING

I had visions and dreams that gave me little droplets of hope. Flying on a magic carpet and landing in foreign places my six-year-old self hadn't heard of before. The magical giant butterfly spirit that came to visit me, and many more. When I shared them with others, they were dismissed. I was made to feel they were only in my head. Being shy and quiet, I got labelled as 'not normal'. I started to slowly shut down and believe the lies.

Fast-forward to nineteen. Flashes came back. Memories deeply buried, silenced. I was unaware I was holding so much accumulated trauma from all the abuses by the so-called 'safe' people I had trusted. I was numb and depressed, though my nineteen-year-old self was unconscious of it. I felt way too much, had no outlet, no tools, no one who understood me, and no safe place.

Having lost faith in God, yet out of a moment of desperation, I resorted to my Catholic upbringing and prayed so hard for my cries to be heard. I learned then that a former childhood friend had received a vision of Christ's heart in the sky. I was silently thinking to myself: "Why haven't I had a vision?" I, too, craved a sign, a miracle. I kept praying as I was in a mess. It was important to me to have faith in something.

Searching for the true meaning of life became my priority. I started to seek answers.

The signs started coming, but in unexpected ways.

What manifested was flashing lights and strange visitors in my dreams. Spacecraft. Colourful beings. A golden being. She was beautiful. A few days later, I walked into a newsagency, grabbed one of those New Age magazines, and there she was — that same golden being with her golden macro braids and piercing eyes.

I thought to myself: "You mean she was real?"

Many more experiences followed. I started buying books on spirituality, practised automatic writing, and learned how to contact the angelic realms. I dived deep into searching for the truth.

I kept all my visions and experiences to myself and decided to move out of home.

During this period of independence, I was put in some awkward and dangerous situations. Too trusting with a stranger led to being stalked and sexually assaulted. I came across some interesting characters, heard and witnessed things I shouldn't have. I learned and experienced a lot during this phase.

I kept searching for my people, then settled into a new faith away from my Catholic upbringing and away from anything New Age. A life of worshipping with rituals seemed to work for me at the time. I thought I had found my home, my people.

Continuing on this safe and sheltered path, something changed. Something shifted. I started seeking help outside this circle. That was when I was forty. I realised these were not my people.

I took action and commenced my healing journey. My deep healing started with Kinesiologists, Mind Body Spirit therapists, all types of hypnotherapy methods including Creatrix and PSH therapy, Astrology, Numerology, psychics, and various healers — searching for answers, for the truth, for the psyche and mind-body-spirit connection, and for what my true destiny was.

I discovered how broken I was, that I had been misled — some would call it brainwashed. I wasn't my own person, but I had held on, thinking it was the only way to Heaven.

I learned about boundaries and grounding for the first time. I discovered I was Autistic and had selective mutism as a child, which explained my struggles — why I was an easy target for bullying and spiritual manipulation, why I was misunderstood throughout my whole life. It explained why I struggled in areas where neurotypical people didn't. I had to learn how to communicate effectively, find my voice, set boundaries, apply self-love and self-care, spot emotional and energy vampires, go to those dark places of the soul for shadow work, and say "no".

During this period, I was swimming in an opposite direction, away from all I had been taught and known. It was a scary world out there with so many new waters and territories yet to be explored, with no instructions or set of rules. I was scared of this newfound freedom. I went through many highs and lows, to hell and back in finding the truth — quite literally in trying to save myself. I landed in very dangerous waters with people who did not care about my wellbeing.

Once more, I saw and witnessed things I shouldn't have.

What I truly yearned for was the need to feel loved, to belong to some community. People need people, even though we are supposed to thrive on our own. We still need support around us that is safe and reliable. What I didn't foresee in the spiritual communities I was yet to cross was that there were some people out there with intentions to harm, manipulate, and abuse. The community I left, although not the truth, ironically felt like the safest option at the time — a security blanket. I did not know then that after I had the courage to leave, I was going to swim in yet another direction, into uncomfortable and unexplored territory.

All I ever searched for was a community where I was loved, supported, seen, heard, and most importantly, felt safe. I did not know who to trust as I came across too many sharks in those waters. I had to find a way to survive and thrive that was healthy and safe. I had to be tossed around a few times during this battle, hitting rock bottom, finding the strength to swim back up again to find the light, my inner light, and see the sun again.

No, I am not being overdramatic. It was really as traumatic as it sounds. It was nothing short of a miracle to pull my way out to the other side.

I am referencing here terrible psychic attacks and people with less than good intentions. I didn't know what was going on or how I was going to pull myself out of it. At times I needed other people to step in. The load I was dealing with was out of this world. I had to fight my way back, work so hard to reclaim my power. It is not a weakness to seek help from other healers. Sometimes we have to take a leap of faith and trust in the extra pair of hands, an extra pair of lenses, as we all have different ways of seeing and different levels of expertise. There are good guardians in this vast human ocean too!

I recognised the people I had unknowingly put on a false pedestal — spiritual figures and various healers. These people I was over-praising did not hold me in such high regard or even respect me. They were not as evolved as I had initially thought. I was viewing them through rose-coloured lenses. This was a cycle that had to be broken in order for me to reclaim my own power.

The ten years that followed were truly my most transformational. I started getting downloads; I started to become the conduit. Only now were my soul gifts ready to resurface.

This is how I found my voice — when I became the channel. My poetry deepened. Channelled messages and stories would flow through my fingertips, through my voice and in foreign tongues (light language). I found a way to deliver messages from nature and beyond. It was a beautiful gift that unfolded. I found my voice and purpose, and it is such an honour to co-create with nature and all of its beings.

Through the various life lessons, I learnt to have more courage and faith in myself, to trust and speak my truth to those who chose to listen through the written word.

I stopped searching for my people. I know they will find me when they are ready and all is aligned.

50th Birthday Revelation

I remember on my 50th birthday, a little over a year ago, I had a dream. An expectant Lyran Feline being, soon to be a mother, stood tall, dressed in a brown hooded gown. She presented me with a book. I flicked through its pages, seeing a story unfold, and realised I was birthing into a new me, birthing a new chapter in my life. It was symbolic of the milestones reached and that I was going to begin a new journey.

This dream gave me hope and showed that I had been supported all along through beings of different realms. It was a very humbling feeling — that someone out there loved me, was supporting me and reminding me of this. It was the best 50th birthday gift.

It was only from being fifty years on this planet that I truly started to realise how far I have come and acknowledge my true power, even though my spiritual awakening started a good while back.

Life indeed is full of surprises. You never know what you are going to get. We have to believe and open up to receive a touch of magic.

Unfolding of the Gift and Moments of Magic

Once, when I did voluntary healings, I discovered much to my amazement that when I was scanning people's bodies, their inner soul tree would reveal itself. Each individual had their own unique soul tree as part of their soul signature, as part of their core. The shape of its trunk, how it branches out, how it roots, fruits it bears highlights the person's soul gifts, personality, creativity, connection with others and the world. How you grow, where it stops and gets disrupted revealing your life traumas, challenges, mother/father issues etc.

I thought — and it is still widely accepted — that our energy flowed the same way, moved in the same direction. But continuously I was shown otherwise. Each individual has their own unique pattern, their own personal rhythm, just like our breath and aura have their own signature.

I felt when this pattern was out of balance. After my sessions, I felt it return to its more natural flow, felt their inner core becoming stronger. I knew deep work had been done when I could feel their core strengthen, new gifts awaken, and when I connected to their soul song.

With my discoveries, I started experimenting. It wasn't deliberate but unfolded spontaneously. I commenced by connecting with my core, then taking deep breaths, being mindful each time, aware of all changes taking place. Most people use 'soul tree' as a brand name to signify deep root healing. But I literally connected to each soul as a tree. We are much more connected to nature than we realise. It cannot be coincidence that whoever came up with mapping our family ancestry used the model of the tree.

With this knowledge, I started to connect more with my inner soul tree to ground myself, connect with my core, and assist with my personal healing. I should have seen it coming — prior to this realisation, I was able to channel messages from trees, flowers, and mushrooms, but also elementals, dragons, and angels. I did not know that trees and nature were going to be so central to my path.

Through my soul tree, the more I went in and dug deep, the deeper I could anchor my roots and feel my core, connecting to my true divine essence. Through my inner soul tree, I connected not only to my most ancient self but to higher realms, to the stars — our eternal tree is our personal bridge to the Earthly and Celestial realms. This enabled me to stay grounded.

Somatically, I practised living in my body, in each part, feeling the presence of my bones, my eyes, then outwardly beyond the body, the space around me, and then even beyond until I felt that oneness, that true connection to nature, to Source. Once this tool was mastered, I would apply it to alleviate pain in whatever part of my body was aching. I would not only bring my awareness to it but talk to it, whisper to it, even sing to it, as I felt it had its own consciousness.

I knew my body could listen. I knew I was shifting in frequency as I could feel the shift. It is like any other tool — the more you practise, the stronger it becomes. I would connect with my core, go within, set the intention to focus on my cosmic body, and really feel it. I felt the light in my body, feeling beyond the flesh and bones, at times as if I was at one with the stars. I literally felt my cosmic body whilst being in my physical vessel, connected to my inner soul tree. In this same space, I would set the intention to commune with my higher self, my oversoul, my inner teacher, my inner shaman. I know when I reached that connection as I could feel the shift in my perception, in my energy, and the wisdom in my words. It felt real. It felt true. It felt like my highest expression.

Moments like these are when I knew I was in my own power, that I had met my authentic self. Finally, I could read beyond the surface of people who crossed my path — those hiding behind layers of masks and camouflage. I could sense and feel what others couldn't.

I found an amazing tool that didn't cost me a thing. This was the best investment of my time and energy.

Let me share some little moments of magic.

I would imagine playing a virtual harp, a celestial harp, knowing exactly how to play it — which string, the right note and melody. It would play without me having learned to play the harp physically, but through my senses alone. All by using my intention and directing it.

I do believe that each of us has those Einstein moments, those moments when a light bulb switches on, when we join the dots and find that missing piece of the puzzle. As we evolve, more souls around the globe will join these dots, completing that puzzle, unravelling one more mystery, one step closer to truth. We all have our own personal book of knowledge within, and our personal soul tree connected to the universal Tree of Life.

From this deep self-realisation, you will find your most authentic self. You will find you are more connected to Source, to nature, than you ever imagined. It is the most empowering feeling when you feel your true core, your true essence.

All gifts of the soul we can harness by knowing how to go within that sacred space, journey through our inner soul tree. We are truly magical instruments of the Divine. The more connected we are, the more threads we can access, the more melodies can be played, and the more we can tune to Source, Divine, God — whatever you want to call it.

We are allowing our inner child to play, to dream again. All your soul gifts will be awakened one by one. You will be more settled in your body, more in flow, more attuned to nature, to the elements, to the universe.

Pearls of Wisdom

Don't blindly follow what others are doing. Tune into your beautiful instrument and listen, feel, find your unique rhythm and flow. Go with the current — you can't have two feet swimming in separate directions. Your soul will guide you where you need to go.

Remember to go slow and at your own pace like the humble snail. Take time to unwind, pause, retreat, and enjoy the nature around you. Make the most of your surroundings and make healthy connections along the way. Maintain that state of flow and balance. Use your time and energy wisely to reach your desired destination. Don't waste your energy arguing your point to someone who is trying to make your life hard. Sometimes remaining quiet, even when you have a lot to say, is the best course of action.

You are who you have been searching for. You have all that you need. You are your own hero.

You are in charge and the key master player in your life. You are a perfect divine instrument as you are. No one can play your instrument better than you.

Korinna Zoya Hunter

Korinna Zoya Hunter is an intuitive channel, poet, spiritual healer and nature empath based in Sydney.

Korinna has a keen eye for spotting beauty around her. In her spare time, she is found not only taking photos of trees and flowers but talking and channelling them too!

Anyone honoured to have a session with Korinna will feel her warmth, her unpretentious caring and non-judgmental nature. You will feel heard, seen and safe. Her passion in assisting you is evident as well as her passion in her craft! Co-creating with nature is her gem!

Korinna is also trauma informed. She is passionate in assisting highly sensitive souls, those confused about their path or who are seeking extra support, guidance and clarity. If her story resonates with you, you can reach Korinna with the following links.

⊕ www.cosmiclightkatalyst.com
❶ www.facebook.com/NovaZoyaAurora
◎ https://wa.me/61452179250

Scan the QR code to learn more about Korinna.

chapter
06

From Grief to Grace
by Sarah Jane Michaels

Life has an individually unique ebb and flow, sometimes like the gentle lapping of waves on the foreshore while in other times like the damaging torrents of a typhoon. What is around the next corner of our human experience may be foreseen and willingly participated in, yet in other moments the secrets of the universe are thickly veiled and we find ourselves thrown into a seemingly uncontrollable reality.

When the vortex of life sucks us down into our darkest of soul-shattering moments, how are we to resurface? How can we become whole once again after feeling as if we have been utterly destroyed? These are the questions and explorations that life prompts.

Let's be honest... the destruction of aspects of our lives isn't really the end. It is a catalyst for the generation of a stronger version of ourselves, where triumph has an opportunity to overcome adversity, resilience can be embodied, personal suffering or catastrophic loss gives way to hope, and new beginnings bloom. The fire that once painfully consumed, now clears way for spiritual clarity and purpose. We transcend from a past state to a more powerful future self.

My own life journey has cycled me through numerous devastating challenges and profound change. At times, I felt as if I was standing amongst crumbled ruins and blackened ashes. The past five years, in particular, have enveloped me with a smokey haze as I faced unfathomable loss. Yet, divine power always brings renewal. I share some of these moments with you as inspiration for your own resurrection from the ashes, just as a Phoenix rises.

The Turning Point Beyond Tragedy

Today, when I awaken in the morning, I love to pause and simply listen to the joyful sounds of birds singing as the dawn's rising sun greets me. I envision my vigour and zest for life. In contrast, I can just as easily recall the darkly haunting mornings when life had zero appeal, when I wondered why I had awakened to the painful reality of another day without my only son.

Aaron was my firstborn of six beautiful children, all raised with a spiritual awareness and respect for their unique life path and soulful gifts. Born at 3.33pm, Aaron was a sensitive soul who embodied the path of 'quiet mastery'. Not an easy life path to traverse, his brain functioned at genius level (ten points above Einstein!), while his body battled the rigours of adulthood epilepsy and addiction.

The unexpected death of Aaron, at a youthful 29 years of age, generated intense waves of shock throughout my entire being. It deeply fractured my psyche and splintered my soul into unrecognisable fragments. I doubted it could ever be rebuilt. I was lost in an unfathomable void — adrift in a life that felt 'unreal'. It was as if pieces of my heart and soul had swiftly left with my son. Aaron was not the only one missing... parts of me were too.

My heart physically 'broke' and began its own life-threatening dysfunctions in response to the devastating grief. Within months, death established a pathway to my own doorstep. One sleepless night, in the blanket of summer heat and in the darkness of my grief, I laid still and quietly gave my body permission to die...

While my son's death was sudden, my own journey toward dangling on the edge of dying would be slow. Failing of the heart can take time, even years. The deep pain of grief and the loss of will to live gradually reshaped my internal heart functions and my personal identity. I was a shadow of my former self — weakened in mind, body and spirit.

Thankfully, the drawn-out nature of this process provided me with the opportunity for experiencing both the challenges of heart-related medical complications and for the miracles of transformative self-healing.

You see, the turning point comes when a powerfully aligned fresh choice to 'live' overrides the previous 'death directive'. Consciousness co-creates reality. Not all of us 'cheat' death. Although, when we do... we have a story to tell.

The Last Hug

When your child rushes out the front door to venture off into an activity, visit friends or catch a train, you never really imagine in that moment that it will be the last time you hug them dearly. As a mother, you simply want to hold them in your embrace for a second longer. You enjoy the moment, hoping they're not going to pull out of your arms too quickly!

A hug between loved ones contains a sweet warmth — in a second your two hearts connect and merge. There's a simple beauty in this shared expression. When it's the very last time you hug this living person, it's a memory that lingers long after they are gone. It's a feeling that is etched deep within your psyche. Somehow, the hug stays with you. It is cherished. I am grateful for my son's last living hug, on the fateful Friday morning he departed our doorstep.

Late into that night's hours an unknown force disturbed my sleep. Awakening, I observed the unusual icy chill enveloping me. A depth of coldness, greater than I had ever experienced, seeped all the way into to my bones. It was a mild spring night, yet I was freezing cold. At odds with my surroundings, the eerie chill felt like an unwanted omen. Something was inexplicably wrong. A deep sadness washed over me as I drifted back into a fitful, restless sleep.

I would later discover, according to police insights, this foreboding moment was the approximate time of my son's passing. A mother and son connected through the ripples of dimensional space, distance and time, still able to touch one another's souls. Such is the mystery and magic of the bond between parent and child.

With the initial numbness and wretchedly distressing days that followed my son's death, I quickly fell into a deep despair. The days were marked with a lonely emptiness, despite having several immediate family members around me and others contactable by phone, (although limited by Covid-related travel restrictions).

Consumed with unrealistic desire, I yearned for my son to reappear at the front door. I simply wanted one more hug. It was the natural longing of a grieving mother. For the intense, elemental link between Aaron and I was broken, leaving me with the internal sounds of anguished screams and silent hurts. The suffering was immense — beyond anything I could have ever imagined.

As the morning light of the third day rose beyond the trees in our small garden, all I could really hope for was a way to reconnect and feel the presence of my son again. The religious symbolism of the third day was not lost to me. A little of my spirit was resurrected. This is when the transformative magic slowly began to weave back into life.

Pledging to Aaron's disembodied consciousness, through my meditative practices while sitting in his garden chair, I offered my full assistance to his journey navigating the immediate afterlife — IF he needed. The motherly role of 'being in service' and nurturing a child's growth was still anchored within me.

While I was deeply rooted in spirituality, with a love of metaphysical science, my son was a self-proclaimed atheist who intellectualised via highly scientific values. (However, I once discovered Aaron levitating in the lotus position as a two-year-old child!) The success of my ability to 'reach' his consciousness was unknown. After all, communicating effectively through the ethers would probably be a steep growth curve for us both.

A swift learner, my son soon engaged in contact through his own initiative. It was a mere few days after his death. I recall walking around the corner of our kitchen and stepping into an invisible, yet seemingly solid, wall. The sensation pushed me backwards, causing a slight loss of balance. This unexpected phenomena brought me to a dead standstill, uncertain of what I had walked into.

The next moments revealed themselves as an all encompassing, warm embrace. I began to feel the liquid-like extensions of energy, as if invisible arms held me firmly. The sensations were similar to those of a tightly squeezing person-to-person hug, bringing a cascade of tears from my eyes. I gratefully received the experience of my son's 'etherial hug.' Our parting physical hug days ago was not the only one he could share with me!

The Release of Light

While my son chose not to align with any singular religious organisation, he always demonstrated a deep respect for both ancient and modern sciences, nature-based holistic practices and the philosophies of Buddhism. Such was his gentle Buddhist-style behaviours, in toddlerhood he could calmly hold a bee between his fingertips and never be stung. As a pre-schooler, when playfully digging in the garden he would carefully move soil to avoid harming earthworms.

Honouring Aaron's body after death, prior to cremation, took careful consideration and planning — especially given the impact of Covid regulations whereby his body would not be released to us for two full weeks, and was only able to be visited by a maximum of eleven people in a single gathering.

My closest friend, a clinical naturopath, had been present at Aaron's birth. It seemed fitting for her to join me in releasing him at death. Together, we journeyed to the funeral home for the first viewing of my son's body. The gravity of sorrow weighed heavily upon us both.

With sacred awareness and spiritual sensitivity, we silently entered the casket room. I was unprepared for the enormity of the confronting sight of my dead child. I broke, buckling at the knees, with wails of despair ringing through the air. My friend's arms circling around me in a quiet strength, I was eventually drawn to my feet. We had a mission to fulfil... the sanctification and blessing of Aaron's body.

Over the period of an hour, together we witnessed him, stood present in his essence and honoured him with non-denominational prayer. In rhythm with my friend's guiding words, and with gentle hands placed on his well-preserved cold body, I anointed Aaron. His head, heart, palms and feet were blessed with the essential oils of rose, lavender, frankincense, sandalwood and myrrh.

Tapping into unseen instincts beyond our everyday lives, it felt as if we were participating in an ancient ritual. Our sacred oils were similar to those of the Myrrhophores (myrrh-bearing priestesses). The intention was to facilitate Aaron's peaceful transition, helping to realign his soul essence for the afterlife ahead.

Intuitively, I moved my hands above his entire body length and core chakras after the anointing of oils. The energetic and slow unwinding of his chakras was to aid his detachment from his body, as his soulful consciousness was still palpable.

When my hands completed the final chakra, I was stunned by the sudden visual of bioluminescence emanating from his body — he was softly glowing! Normally extremely faint, ultra-weak photon emission (UPE) is a side effect of energy metabolism. The happening before my eyes was both mysterious and mystical. My scientific knowledge was forced to bridge into spiritual possibilities.

Next, in an awe-inspiring display, photons of light particles burst from his entire body, rising upward! While I knew photons could be seen by the naked eye, never before had I witnessed such magnificence from the deceased. Tears streamed down my face as I called out to my friend, "Look at the light, look at the light... It's so beautiful." Our work was done. My son was free to journey into new dimensions.

As we exited the funeral home, we were farewelled by the gentle-faced director. He paused to share the profoundly meaningful words, "The two of you have the gift of communing with the dead. Aaron's soul is blessed by what you have done for him." I was both flabbergasted and delighted by the director's parting comments. It appeared he knew the secrets of the deceased.

Signs from the Universe

My deep longing for connection beyond the physical realm, and finding meaning in symbolism, often led to personally significant encounters or experiences in the months ahead. The varied forms of after-death communication (ADCs) phenomena provided me with a small measure of comfort, reassurance and a continued sense of presence throughout the toughest bereavement phases. Aaron's siblings were also privy to a range of signs from the universe. Each afterlife message reassured us that our beloved Aaron was still present in spirit.

In particular, I was gifted with validations via apparitions, vivid dream visitations, sensing Aaron's presence moving toward me, and even feeling movement as if he sat on the bed beside me. With an uncanny frequency, I witnessed repetitive and unexplained electrical disturbances while I was thinking of Aaron, erratic electronic device functions, and sudden activations from Aaron-related apps on my phone — some even indicating he was 'last seen' one minute ago!

The natural occurrences of nature further contributed to the interpretations of spiritual signs. Aaron held a fascination and an appreciation for ants, so it was no surprise that densely populated trails of black ants gravitated around my feet during Aaron-focused meditations.

Black and white butterflies often drifted toward us, flying exceptionally close. We first encountered these winged messengers when my family gathered in the bushy banks of a river near the site of Aaron's death, adjacent to a University. We were compelled to sit in the precise location of his passing — to feel 'something' of his last moments.

My eldest daughter led the way through the scrub, trees and long grasses. The inner compass of connection to her brother guiding her footsteps. Without any fear of snakes, she moved with solid focus and intention to find his yoga mat where he laid to rest, deep in the brush.

Thankfully, it was left behind by police and the three students who discovered Aaron's body — serving as our crucial landmark.

Spreading ourselves in a close-knit circle, we sat with his blue mat. Each of our faces distorted with grief, we held a silent vigil before moving into simple rituals suitable for Aaron's younger siblings. As we shared memories of Aaron, each of us marvelled at the unexpected visitation of flittering black and white butterflies. They danced in circles closely over each of our heads, as if to kiss the air above our hair! For young and older alike, the butterflies symbolised Aaron's spiritual presence — bringing us comforting messages of hope in his soul's transformation and endurance.

Liberation from the Void

Time and time again, my morning meditations and channelling links with Aaron proved light-filled and positive. However, as the weeks passed, a subtle shift in his soulful consciousness indicated his growing struggles. He was not at peace. With the sudden trauma of his death, unresolved issues at play and spiritual wounds, it became evident that Aaron genuinely needed help journeying through the afterlife.

While alive, Aaron developed an affinity to shamanism. In honour of his interests, I sought the support of a local Native American Indian Shaman. I was gifted with wise counsel, musical rhythms of drums and healing bodywork.

Never before had I experienced the process of grief being released from my cellular tissues via the rhythmical percussion of hands. The Shaman skilfully beat a vibrating pulse through my upper back, chest and pericardium. Emotions swelled, bubbling upward with rolling tears. My grief could not be contained.

Feeling clearer, I was ready to be guided into the 'void' to compel Aaron to leave his dark, self-imposed confines and return to a 'higher plane' where the joyous realms of light existed. Clasping the hand of the Shaman, together we psychically dove into the void to locate Aaron. It was both unsettling and disturbing. An array of disembodied beings swirled chaotically, trapped in their own lower vibrations. It was a torturous realm.

With powerful words scripted in native chants and aligned intentions, the Shaman and I directed Aaron to the edge of the void. My son needed to surrender his remnants of lower ego and pain, to make the final choice to 'cross over' into the expansiveness of the universe, the godly place of pure love and light.

I later enlisted family members far and wide, regardless of their beliefs, to support Aaron in fully crossing over. It was a blessing that so many people, particularly my devoted mother, were willing to learn the native chants and prayers to support Aaron's transition. My gratitude was deeply felt for their generous responsiveness to such unfamiliar customs.

Maintaining our family connection across oceans, other countries and even astral realms, felt like a final act of love for Aaron. United, we had guided him toward liberation and ensured his soul's well-being.

Days later, in our 'mother and son' dawn meditations, Aaron confirmed his evolutionary leap beyond earthly limitations. He revealed to me the magnificence of his metamorphosis and omnipresence. It was a truly astounding and joyous insight into his divine nature.

Wounds of the Heart

Despite the releasing rituals and deep family conversations, the well-being of our own hearts remained comprised. This was particularly true for my mother and I, as we mirrored each other with physical heart complications following the shock of Aaron's death and the unending days of grief.

THE SOUL'S RISING

For both mother and grandmother, broken Heart Syndrome (Takotsubo Cardiomyopathy) progressed to long-term health issues, weakened heart muscles, bradycardia, heart attack symptoms and even progressive heart failure in my mother.

Five days into one of my hospitalisations, I recall the striking moments of my cardiologist emphatically saying, "You could drop dead tomorrow!" Clearly, it was time for me to HEAL.

For two hours, in the privacy of my hospital room with the door solidly closed, I created a 'sound bath'. The etherial music and Vedic chants I played on audio were designed to assist me in repairing my human heart. As the sound waves echoed, filling the entire room, I fully embraced the purpose of self-healing. Using creative visualisation, bio-energy work and spiritual healing, I began the process of 'etherically' repairing my heart. The will to survive and thrive became a clear choice.

It was six months later, in a hospital follow-up assessment, that I considered the possibility of a miracle having occurred. Frankly, some words remain etched in our minds. This is certainly true of my assessing cardiologist's statement, "There is no sign of any previous recorded damage. You are a medical mystery!"

In the roller-coaster months and years following such unimaginable loss, healing does not arrive as a finish line, but as a series of small, brave choices to keep living while carrying love forward. Grief may never disappear, yet it can soften, making room for moments of breath, meaning, peace and even self-evolution.

A broken heart can learn a new rhythm — one that honours a loved one's life, (not only his or her absence), and allows memory to co-exist with hope. By tending gently to the body, the mind, and the spirit, it becomes possible to rise each day with the truth that love did not end with death. It continues — in the stories told, the kindness extended, and the quiet strength found in surviving, one step at a time.

Life is truly worth living, and there is light at the end of the tunnel. That light is the purest of loves. It is Divine.

Sarah Jane Michaels

Sarah Jane is an internationally respected metaphysical healer, integrative wellness practitioner and student Doctor of Ayurveda. With over 30 years of experience supporting deep, lasting transformation, she blends ancient wisdom with modern neuroscience and bioenergetics to address healing at the root cause. Working holistically across the physical, emotional, mental and energetic levels, Sarah Jane helps people reconnect with their body's innate wisdom and natural state of harmony.

Qualified in Ayurveda, holistic nutrition, metaphysical healing, body harmony, somatic bodywork, kinesiology, and neuro-transformation coaching, Sarah Jane's evidence-informed and multi-faceted approach empowers clients to release long-held patterns, restore balance, and activate their innate capacity for wellness.

Sarah Jane's work has been featured in global media and radio, and she serves a diverse, world-wide client base. A 10-time #1 International Bestselling Author, she is known for creating profound shifts where traditional methods fall short — guiding others to heal deeply and return home to themselves with clarity, vitality and purpose.

⊕ www.wellnessworld.life
❶ www.facebook.com/sarahjanemichaels/
Scan the QR code to learn more about Sarah.

chapter 07

Dimensions and Timelines Through the Eyes of Self

by Carola Werth

The Universe Within: An Invitation

Remember, the Universe is not something separate from you; it is a vast, breathing reality that exists within us all. We are currently standing at the precipice of a monumental evolution — entering a beautiful, yet often daunting, journey of becoming Universal Humans.

This transition is a heartfelt inner knowing, a quiet hum in the soul that grows louder as we begin to remember who we really are. However, it is also a journey that can feel profoundly confusing and lonely. As we step into the uncharted waters of self-discovery, we are forced to confront just how powerful we truly are. It is a weight that not everyone is ready to carry. You must remember: there is no 'wrong' or 'right' way to walk this path. This is your personal growth, your unique soul-contract, and your own timing. We are being asked to bridge the gap between our physical existence and our eternal nature, a feat that requires us to look directly into the mirror of the soul without flinching.

The Canals of My Childhood

Spiritual awakening is not a singular event that happens at a specific time; it is a tapestry that starts being woven the moment we are born. For me, the search for belonging began early. I was always searching — to be 'good enough' in a world that constantly directs our gaze outward, teaching us to measure our worth by the reflections in other people's eyes.

My earliest memories are anchored in Germany, living near a canal. The atmosphere was often heavy, but for me, the veil was incredibly thin. Even as a small child, I was already seeing spirit. While other children were focused on toys and games, I was witnessing the profound and often traumatic departure of souls.

I can still recall the chilling stillness of accidents by the canal. What stood out most vividly wasn't the tragedy itself, but the sight of the soul leaving the physical body. I would watch, mesmerised, as a shimmering essence would float above a deceased person, detached and peaceful, while the world below was in chaos. These spirits were my first teachers. In those moments, I understood that death was not a wall, but a doorway. To me, talking to these beings was as natural as breathing, though I soon learned that the rest of the world did not see through the same lens. I had to learn to keep my observations to myself, creating a secret world within me where the 'unseen' was more real than the 'seen.'

A New Land and the Fracturing of Self

In 1973, at the age of twelve, my life was uprooted. We moved to Australia. I remember the shock of the light — it was so much brighter and harsher than the soft greys of Germany. The vastness of the Australian landscape was intimidating, a reflection of the internal space I was beginning to navigate. But as the external landscape expanded, my internal world began to fracture.

The shift into my teenage years was marked by the painful divorce of my parents. The stability I had known evaporated, replaced by a deep family confusion that I wasn't equipped to handle. By the age of fourteen, I ran away. I ended up in foster care, and it was there that I made a conscious, albeit subconscious, choice to walk the hard road. The 'wild child' within me took over. Rebellious and hurting, I decided to explore the dark side of the soul. I felt like an outsider in a world governed by rigid rules I couldn't understand.

I had to learn to grow up fast. I saw the ugliest sides of humanity — the cruelty, the manipulation, and the coldness of a system that often felt like it had no heart. I often wondered why we existed in such a harsh reality. Many times, the 'victim' in me was the only part that felt real. Yet, looking back, I see that I was never truly alone. Even in my darkest moments of despair, an angel would appear — sometimes as a spirit, sometimes as a kind stranger who offered a meal or a place to sleep — to guide me back toward a better way. These were the breadcrumbs left by the Universe to ensure I didn't lose my way entirely.

Lessons from the Pit

My life has been marked by many 'bottom-of-the-pit' moments. These were the times when the weight of the world felt like it would crush me, yet they were also the moments that taught me the most profound lessons about love.

I spent years being seduced by fear. I sought out adventures that I thought would make me feel alive, but they only brought unbearable heartache. This cycle was fuelled by a deep-seated belief that I was not worthy of anything better. I attracted people who reflected my own brokenness back to me, creating a loop of trauma that felt inescapable. But as I eventually learned, my pain was my gain. It was the fuel for my transformation. These traumatic experiences established a bridge between me and the spiritual beings in the unseen world. They were watching, waiting for me to realise that I could use my sensitivity as a tool rather than a burden.

I have had near-death experiences where I was allowed to go 'home' to a place of absolute, unconditional love. In that space, there is no time, no judgment, and no pain. Each time, I felt the pull to stay in that frequency — to remain in the place I call home. Yet, I chose to come back. I chose to return to this physical body to overcome my fear, to believe in my own light, and to learn how to be my authentic self in a world of masks. I realised that I hadn't finished what I came here to do.

The Trauma Closet

The path of awakening is like peeling an onion. You think you have healed a layer, only to find something deeper that requires your attention. We all have what I call a 'trauma closet.' Some of us are ready to open the door and let the light in, while others keep it locked for lifetimes.

In my younger years, I was a broken woman. I had a daughter at a time when I barely knew how to care for myself. Her father's life ended in a way that haunted me for decades. He was a roadie for the bands Cold Chisel and Swanee, a life of constant movement and music. One day, while he was sleeping in the back of a truck, a horrific accident occurred. Two people died that day, and my world shattered along with them.

For years, I carried the crushing weight of guilt. My daughter grew up with her grandparents, and the distance between us felt like a physical wound. I kept blaming myself, replaying the 'what ifs' in a loop that kept me anchored to the past. It took a long time to heal that specific trauma. If I'd had the spiritual tools that I have today, I would have handled it differently — but that is the nature of the journey. We learn through the struggle.

Forgiving oneself is the greatest hurdle we face. We see our children hurt and feel helpless; we see loved ones pass over and feel abandoned. Yet, through this, we become stronger. Our survival is not just about staying alive; it's about thriving in spite of the scars. Every scar is a map of where we have been and a testament to the fact that we are still here.

The Shift in Consciousness

We are currently witnessing a global 'split' in consciousness. On one side, we have the old consciousness — a dying system still clutching at fear, control, and karmic debt. You see it in the political arenas of every nation. These systems work tirelessly to keep you tethered to fear, much like religious institutions did in centuries past. They want you to believe you are small, separate, and powerless.

This old way of being taught us to look outside of ourselves for solutions. It created a culture of victims and finger-pointing. But the 'shadow' is now serving a purpose; it is acting as the catalyst for many to finally stand up and take their power back.

The new consciousness is the antithesis of the old. It is built on the pillars of self-love, kindness, and personal responsibility. It is about unlearning the patterns of blame and hatred that have been passed down through generations. To move into this new frequency, we must look at our 'unseen emotions'— the frequencies within us that have been exploited by outside forces. We are often taught to hate people we've never met and to fear a future that hasn't happened. Our minds are filled with visions of being 'not enough,' which is the ultimate tool of control.

Many people are now walking away from these lower vibrations. Some call this the 'Splitting of the Earth' or the opening of 'Stargates.' Whatever you call it, it is a movement toward a higher vibration where we realise that we are, and always have been, worthy. We are shifting from 'doing' to 'being.'

Starting Over at Fifty

My true 'Great Awakening' happened when I moved to the Gold Coast. I had built a life — I had a house, a stable environment, and I was attending spiritual churches and events. I was 'doing the work,' or so I thought. I completed certificates in various healing modalities, yet there was a lingering sense that I was still missing a piece of the puzzle. I was collecting knowledge, but I wasn't yet embodying it.

During one profound healing session, a practitioner looked at me and said, "You need to bring your soul back into your body." It was a shock. My soul was so fractured from my past traumas that parts of me were literally scattered across different timelines. That was the moment I truly committed to the healing journey. I began to understand that healing isn't just about fixing what is broken; it's about reclaiming the parts of ourselves we left behind in moments of pain.

Then, life tested me. In my fifties, when most people are looking toward retirement and stability, I was called to give it all up. I outgrew a twenty-year relationship and moved to Hervey Bay. I sold my home, and for a traumatic few months, I was broke and technically homeless.

But when you surrender to the flow, the Universe provides. A 'human angel' appeared and rented me a beautiful room until I could afford my own place. Another angel lent me the money to move my furniture while I waited for the house settlement. It was overwhelming to start again at that age, but it was necessary. In the stillness of that new beginning, my gifts exploded. I began channelling artwork and drawing Light Language. My healing sessions became more powerful as I received direct downloads and visions. I learned that we outgrow people and places not as a punishment, but as an invitation to find our true inner strength. I realised that my 'home' was not a building, but the frequency I carried within me.

The Rebalancing of Energy

A critical part of our mission as humans is the rebalancing of masculine and feminine energies. For too long, the feminine energy has been under attack. This suppression has caused a distortion in the masculine — leading to disrespect, ego-driven control, and a low-vibrational 'survival mode.' We see this in the way we treat the Earth and the way we treat each other.

To enter the new consciousness, we must harmonise these energies within ourselves. The masculine must become the protector of the feminine, providing the structure and safety for the feminine to bloom. The feminine must be allowed to lead with intuition, heart, and creation. This is not about gender; it is about frequency. Every part of our sacred self has been under immense stress, but our inner strength has led us to this point of rebalance. When these two energies meet in harmony within the heart, we become whole.

Working with the Unseen Guides

My work in the unseen world is supported by a team of incredible beings from other galaxies and dimensions. They are always willing to help, provided you are ready to ask and absorb the information. They do not intervene without permission, as they respect our free will, but they are ever-present.

I want to acknowledge my guides: Ulexis, from the planet Arcturus, who introduced me to the Pleiadian Brothers, Master Chuan Lee, and Sananda. Together, they form a team that has taken me on adventures across dimensions. They taught me how to trust myself and how to ignore the judgment of others.

Through them, I learned to draw Stargates with specific codes — geometric keys that unlock higher frequencies. When I draw these, I feel a surge of energy through my arm, as if the pen is being moved by a force beyond my own. These codes act as anchors for light, helping people to shift their vibration almost instantly. I learned how to 'unhook' souls from ancient traumas — literally seeing the energetic cords that tie people to their past — and how to mend the heart space across multiple lifetimes.

I remember a tall, vibrant blue being, who felt like Archangel Michael, appearing to me while holding a soul. Telepathically, he asked me if I was ready to take on my mission to help mend these fractured spirits. I said yes, and in that moment, my path was sealed. I began to see people not as their problems, but as the beautiful, eternal souls they truly are.

Rescue Missions in the Night

When your soul travels into the night in your dream state, you are often doing more than just resting. Some of us are called to rescue missions — helping souls pass over during world disasters or accidents. I have had incredibly clear visions of being in a 'between-worlds' space, guiding confused and frightened souls toward the light.

During world events, I feel the collective grief, and my soul goes into service. I have seen myself standing at the edge of a great transition, holding space for those who have left their bodies suddenly. It is a sacred duty, one that requires a deep level of trust in the unseen. When I wake up, I often feel a profound sense of peace, knowing that I have helped someone find their way home. This is the work of a Universal Human — being of service across the seen and unseen worlds.

Protection: Navigating the Shadows

Because I work so closely with the unseen, I have learned the importance of protection. The unseen world is not always 'love and light.' It contains the full spectrum of energy. In my twenties, I was attacked in my sleep by a vicious, animal-like entity. It was a terrifying experience that taught me that our energy field must be sealed. Years later, a dark entity tried to choke me, an experience that forced me to reclaim my voice and my power. Even in the 'seen' world, we encounter energy vampires and narcissistic manipulation.

I use tea tree oil as a tool for remote viewing; its vibration is something lower beings cannot tolerate. I place a few drops on my shoulder blades, where our 'etheric wings' are said to be, to seal my energy field against intrusion.

For those of you beginning your own channelling or healing work, I offer this practice. It is simple, but powerful:

1. *Breathe:* Three deep breaths to settle your nervous system and bring you into the present moment.
2. *Ground:* Imagine roots extending from your feet deep into the crystalline layer of Mother Earth. Feel her stability.
3. *Invoke:* Declare your space with authority. "I invoke the light. I am God within. I am a clear and perfect channel. Pure energy from my highest good will guide me through safely. I allow myself to align to the higher frequency. I keep out the negative and enter into the quantum field with light being my guide. I am pure. My connection is pure."
4. *Seal:* "And so it is. And so it is. And so it is."

Stepping into the New

I am the navigator of my journey. I am constantly undoing the old consciousness to make room for the new. I raise my frequency and align with the rhythm of the Universal Monad — the source of all that is. The Monad is the original spark of divinity from which we all came, and returning to its rhythm is the ultimate goal of our evolution.

Repeat these affirmations to yourself, and feel them in your cells:

- I am the God/Goddess energy who brings balance back.
- I am the masculine and the feminine, learning unconditional acceptance.
- I am the Monad, the Universal Source of all existence harmonised by the Divine.
- I am an eternal soul.
- I am consciousness.

Taking a new direction is rarely easy. We are wired to seek the comfort of the familiar, even if the familiar is painful. It takes courage to step into the unknown. But I ask you: Are you ready to be free of fear? Are you ready to let go of the stories that have kept you small?

THE SOUL'S RISING

I am one of those souls that needs to understand the darkness — to know how we ended up in these strange, repeating cycles of trauma and control. While the old world still has a strong hold on the minds of many, deep in my soul, I am excited. We are the magical beings tasked with bringing back the harmony of peace. That is our mission. It is unfolding in every breath, in every choice, and in every moment we choose love over fear. We are the ones we have been waiting for.

Carola Werth

Carola Werth is the heart and soul behind Soul Mender, based in beautiful Hervey Bay, Queensland. For over 40 years, Carola has walked between worlds as a Psychic Medium, Spiritual Healer, and Teacher, supporting souls to find clarity, heal what has been fractured, and reconnect with loved ones beyond the veil.

Through the Looking Glass Oracle Deck, Soul Mending sessions, and her teachings, Carola offers practical tools to release old patterns, balance energies, and awaken innate spiritual gifts. Her work flows through oracle and tarot readings, energetic healing, and channelled guidance.

Carola channels divine wisdom from higher realms including Arcturus, the Pleiadians, Sananda, Chung Lee, Merlin, and Archangel Michael. Her work features in OracleME Magazine and across YouTube, Facebook, and the global spiritual community.

Her mission is simple yet profound: to remind you that you were never alone — and the veil is thinning for those ready to see.

⊕ www.soulmendercarola.com
❶ www.facebook.com/carola.werth.56
◉ www.instagram.com/carola8998

Scan the QR code to learn more about Carola.

chapter 08

When Spirit Entered My Life and Cracked Me Open

by Melissa Paris

Spirit entered my life long before I had language for it. Long before I knew words like intuition, medium, psychic, or gift. Before fear learned how to speak louder than wonder.

As a child, I didn't feel tethered to the earth the way others seemed to be. My body was here, but my soul felt elsewhere. Lighter, wider, listening. I felt more connected to the stars than the ground beneath my feet, as though part of me belonged somewhere beyond this world, somewhere vast and quiet and endlessly watching.

While other children played inside, I would lie on the grass at night, eyes fixed on the sky, feeling held by something unseen. The stars felt like old friends. Familiar. Safe. They didn't ask questions. They didn't judge. They simply existed, steady and constant, reminding me that there was more than what I could see during the day.

It was under those stars that I spoke to my father.

He passed away before my first birthday, yet he was never absent to me. I was born on his birthday, an echo, a continuation, a strange and sacred thread that stitched us together across the veil. I didn't know him in the way others knew their fathers. I didn't know the sound of his voice in the physical world or the weight of his hand holding mine. But I felt him. Deeply. Constantly. As if his presence lived just beyond the edges of my vision, close enough to touch if I leaned into the quiet.

I didn't feel safe talking to my mother. She felt distant, like a stranger, emotionally unavailable in ways I only fully understood later in life.

So I would look to the stars and talk to my dad out loud. I would cry to him, tell him about my day, my thoughts, my fears, my pain, my small victories. I would ask him questions. I remember one question I asked him: "Why am I here?" I didn't question whether he could hear me. I knew he could. I would also receive answers, which always made me feel closer. There was no doubt in my body, no separation in

THE SOUL'S RISING

my mind. He felt closer to me in death than many people felt to their loved ones in life.

Even then, spirit was already walking beside me.

I could see things others couldn't. Hear things no one else reacted to. Feel shifts in rooms, in people, in energy that had no visible source. At times, it was beautiful, a sense of being guided, protected, seen. At times, it was terrifying.

I saw spirits, not as dramatic apparitions, but as presences. Impressions. Shapes in the periphery. Faces that appeared when no one else was there. I heard voices that weren't my own, whispers that carried emotion more than sound. I felt emotions that weren't mine crash into my body without warning. Grief, fear, longing, pain flooding me as if my nervous system had no filter.

As a child, I didn't understand boundaries. I didn't know how to turn it off. Spirit didn't knock. It entered.

When you're young, unprotected, and sensitive, that can feel like drowning.

There were nights I was afraid to sleep. Afraid of what I might see when I closed my eyes. Afraid of what might come closer in the dark. Afraid of how real it all felt. I didn't know how to explain what I was experiencing, and when I tried, the reactions taught me quickly that this wasn't safe to share.

I learned silence early.

I learned that seeing too much made people uncomfortable. That knowing things without explanation made me strange. That feeling deeply was not rewarded but punished. So I began to shrink. To fold myself inward. To doubt what my body and soul knew instinctively.

Leaving Home

I became homeless at fourteen. It was the last time my mother tried to physically abuse me. That was the day I stood up to her and took my power back.

I went from couch to couch. I stayed with my aunty for a while, then I met a married man and became pregnant at the age of fourteen. He let me stay there for a short period of time, then told me I had to go. I didn't understand why at the time. I later came to realise he was married when my uncle recognised him after he dropped me off at home.

I got kicked out of my aunty's house. They said I was a bad influence on my cousins. I was homeless again and pregnant.

I turned to my mum because I felt really low and alone. She didn't encourage me. She told me to get an abortion and that they would not support me at all if I chose to have the baby. She wasn't supportive anyway, so what was I expecting?

I was homeless. I couldn't go back home. The dread got deeper. I couldn't look after myself properly, let alone a child. Abortions went against what I believed in. I didn't know what to do.

I then met a new partner and he was very supportive. He said he would support me no matter what I decided and he would raise the child as his own. The father told me to get rid of it and he would pay. My mum contacted me again, and by that time I had agreed to have an abortion. Every part of me was fighting, but I knew it wasn't fair to bring a child into this world when I was struggling myself.

I made the appointment. My mother told me to tell the father it cost money, even though it was free. He paid the said amount.

As I lay in the hospital bed ready to do the one thing I really didn't want to do, my mum turned to me and said, "Do you have the money he gave you?" I said yes. Then she asked to borrow it so she could go to the pokies. She assured me she would be back by the time I got out of surgery.

Again I was left feeling isolated and alone.

When I was being taken in for surgery, I was crying uncontrollably.

The nurses were lovely and tried to keep me calm. Just before going under, I went to say stop, I don't want this, but it was too late. They couldn't understand me properly. I went to sleep.

When I woke up, my mum was nowhere to be seen and my baby was gone.

Afterwards, I was focusing on where I was going to go now. I finally sought help. I was put into residential care where I had a room. Many strangers around, but it was a space I called my own for a while at least. A few months later I was offered youth housing, along with one other girl.

The Weight of Growing Up

As I grew older, life layered trauma on top of sensitivity. Childhood wounds. Abandonment. Loss. Grief that was never fully named or processed. I lost friends, far too many, far too young. Some to crime, some to drugs, some to illness. Each death left a mark on me. Each one changed me, little by little, leaving spaces inside my heart where love and loss lived side by side.

Every funeral felt familiar, as if I had been there before. While the pain was real and heavy, I always felt connected. I could feel them, sense them, hear them, see them. Death never felt like an ending. It felt like a shift. A doorway.

Still, the weight accumulated. Toxic relationships mirrored the chaos I hadn't yet healed. My nervous system lived in survival mode. My mind became loud, harsh, relentless.

My first real intimate relationship ended in betrayal. Infidelity shattered what little safety I had learned to cling to. There was emotional abuse that slowly eroded my sense of self, and in my own unhealed pain, I became physically abusive in moments. I did not yet have the tools to regulate. That relationship was a collision of wounds, two people in survival, replaying patterns neither of us understood at the time. I carry accountability for who I was then, without shame, knowing now that harm often grows where pain goes unhealed.

My second relationship was darker. Mentally, emotionally, and physically abusive, it stripped me of my sense of autonomy and safety entirely. I lived in fear. I fled. I moved from refuge to refuge, carrying my life in pieces, learning what it meant to survive rather than live. That period fractured me, but it also planted the earliest seeds of self-preservation. I learned that love should never require disappearance.

By the time I entered my third relationship, something in me had begun to shift. It has been deeply healing, though not without its lessons. It has asked me to unlearn survival, to recognise safety, to soften where I once braced for impact. Through it, I have learned what repair looks like. What growth feels like. What it means to choose differently rather than repeat patterns unconsciously.

Each relationship reflected where I was in my healing at the time. None were wasted. All were teachers.

Shutting Down

At this stage of my life, I sought professional help and received mental health diagnoses that helped explain what my nervous system had been carrying for years.

Spirit, once gentle and present, became overwhelming. Instead of feeling guided, I felt invaded. Instead of feeling supported, I felt exposed.

I was called crazy. Too sensitive. Unstable. Delusional. Labels landed like stones, and eventually, I picked them up and used them against myself.

So I did what I thought I had to do to survive. The noise of the wounds had become overwhelming in my body and mind.

I shut it down.

I built walls inside my mind and heart. I numbed myself. I ignored the sensations, dismissed the signs, pushed away the knowing. I told myself it wasn't real. That I had imagined it. That I was broken and needed to be fixed.

And for a long time, that worked, at least on the surface. But shutting down spirit also meant shutting down parts of myself.

My intuition dulled. My creativity dimmed. My sense of meaning faded. I felt disconnected not only from spirit, but from me. I existed, but I wasn't alive.

There was a darkness in that period of my life, not dramatic, but heavy. A low-grade despair that hummed beneath everything. Trauma sat in my body like a silent witness, influencing my thoughts, my choices, my relationships. I repeated patterns because they felt familiar, even when they hurt. I wasn't listening to my soul anymore.

Eventually, something inside me reached its limit.

The Long Road Back

I didn't return to spirituality right away. In fact, I did the opposite. I turned towards my mind, towards psychology, healing, trauma work, self-awareness. Somewhere deep inside, I knew that before I could open back up to spirit, I needed to feel safe inside myself.

So I committed to my healing. Not for a year. Not for a phase. For over a decade. I did the hard, unglamorous work. I faced my trauma instead of bypassing it. I challenged my thoughts. I learned emotional regulation. I unpacked belief systems that weren't mine. I rebuilt my relationship with myself piece by piece.

There were setbacks. Relapses into old patterns. Moments where I questioned whether any of it was worth it.

But I stayed.

And slowly, something changed. My mind became quieter. My nervous system softened. My inner world stabilised. It was only then, when I felt more whole, more grounded, that curiosity began to return.

At first, it was subtle. A pull I couldn't explain. Dreams that felt different, clearer, more intentional. I started noticing signs again. Numbers. Songs. Feelings of presence. That familiar sensation of being watched over, not in a threatening way, but in a protective one.

Spirit hadn't left. It had waited.

Still, I hesitated. Fear lingered. I remembered how overwhelming it once was, how alone I had felt. I wasn't sure I was ready to open that door again.

Cracked Open

And then, in 2017, everything changed.

My mother passed away. Nothing prepared me for that loss.

I was pregnant at the time, carrying life while preparing to say goodbye to the woman who had anchored me to this world. Grief cracked me open in a way nothing else ever had. Losing her felt like losing the last tether to the physical. The woman who had known me my entire life, who had seen every version of me, was suddenly gone.

I held myself together for my baby. I had to. I went into labour the day of her funeral. My body carried both death and life in the same breath. I stood at her farewell while contractions rippled through me, grief and creation entwined in the most surreal, sacred way.

After my baby was born, the ground fell out from under me. The grief hit like a tidal wave. Raw. Immersive. Consuming. I had so many unanswered questions. So much left unsaid. I spiralled into a darkness deeper than anything I had known before. Postpartum vulnerability collided with loss, and for a time, I felt lost inside my own life.

But even then, especially then, spirit arrived.

Within minutes of my mother's passing, I received a sign. It wasn't subtle. It wasn't symbolic. It was precise. Personal. Unmistakable. The kind of sign that doesn't ask for belief. It demands recognition.

Spirit didn't ease me back in gently. It cracked me open.

Becoming the Bridge

After my mother crossed over, my connection to spirit deepened in ways I could no longer ignore.

It was as if a door had been flung open inside me. Messages came through more clearly. Sensations sharpened. My intuition became precise, undeniable. I began to understand that my grief had not broken me. It had initiated me.

I started to see that every loss I had endured had been shaping me. Each friend I lost. Each goodbye that never felt final. Each moment of standing between worlds without realising it. All of it was preparation.

I began to hone my abilities intentionally instead of fighting them. I studied, practised, and learned how to ground myself so I wouldn't be consumed by what I felt. I learned discernment, how to open and close the door, how to protect my energy, how to listen without drowning.

Mediumship became more than something that happened to me. It became something I chose.

I realised that being a psychic medium wasn't about death. It was about love. It was about continuity. It was about reminding people that their loved ones are not gone, only transformed.

Mediumship became my passion because I know grief intimately. I know the ache of unanswered questions. I know the desperation to feel them one more time. I know the pain of carrying on when part of your heart exists somewhere else.

When I sit with someone in their grief, I don't stand above it. I stand inside it with them. I become the bridge so they don't feel so alone in that space. I translate what spirit wants them to know. I help bring comfort, clarity, and healing where there was once only pain.

As an energy healer, I see how trauma, loss, and suppression lodge themselves in the body. I feel where energy is blocked, where grief has hardened, where fear has taken root.

I no longer question why I was born sensitive. I no longer resent what I can feel. I no longer see my path as a burden. I see it as sacred.

I understand now that my father has walked with me my entire life. That my mother did not leave me. She expanded beyond form. That those I have lost continue to guide, protect, and love from the other side.

I was not broken. I was opened.

Spirit cracked me open so I could become a vessel. So I could hold space for others when they feel like they're falling apart. So I could stand between worlds and say: You are still loved. You are still connected. You are not alone.

This is not a role I take lightly. It is a responsibility. An honour. A calling. And it is one I embrace.

I work as a psychic medium to remind people that love does not die.

Spirit doesn't shout anymore. It whispers. And I listen.

Looking Back

Spirit entered my life long ago, but it was through loss, healing, grief, and love that it finally cracked me open and taught me how to stay.

Looking back now, I can recognise how all of this lived in my body long before I had the words for it. There was a constant tension in my chest, a sense of alertness that never fully switched off. I often felt tired without knowing why, emotionally full before the day had even begun. I noticed things others didn't seem to notice, changes in mood, energy, tone, and I learned early that it was easier to observe quietly than to explain myself.

THE SOUL'S RISING

I also carried a deep sense of responsibility from a young age, as though I needed to hold things together even when I didn't understand what was falling apart. I felt things intensely and personally. When someone around me was hurting, my body reacted as if it were my own pain. At the time, I thought this was weakness. I didn't realise it was sensitivity without support.

Loss shaped how I moved through the world. It made me careful, hyper-aware, and at times emotionally guarded. But it also made me compassionate in a very real way. I became someone who could sit with discomfort without trying to rush past it. Someone who could stay present when things were messy, heavy, or unresolved.

Healing wasn't a breakthrough moment. It was repetitive and often frustrating. It looked like learning to pause instead of react. Like noticing when my body was in fight or flight. Like choosing safer patterns even when chaos felt familiar. There were days I doubted myself and days I felt proud simply for staying.

Over time, I began to feel more settled in myself. More anchored. The connection I once feared no longer overwhelmed me because I had learned how to ground, how to regulate, how to stay present in my body. Spirit no longer pulled me away from my life. It fit into it.

What once felt like too much became manageable. What once felt confusing became clearer. And what once felt isolating became a point of connection.

I didn't arrive here by bypassing my experiences.

I arrived here by working through them, one grounded step at a time.

Melissa Paris

Melissa Paris is an intuitive guide, psychic medium and spiritual mentor devoted to helping people reconnect with their inner truth, strength and soul wisdom. Her journey has been shaped by deep healing, personal transformation and a lifelong connection to energy and spirit, experiences that allow her to guide others with empathy, clarity and grounded insight.

Blending intuition with practical guidance, Melissa offers messages that empower rather than predict, encouraging self-trust, emotional healing and conscious choice. Her work supports those navigating awakening, relationships, trauma recovery and life transitions, helping them move from survival into alignment.

Through intuitive readings, guidance videos, mediumship and spiritual education, Melissa creates a safe, empowering space where insight meets action. Her message is simple yet powerful: healing is possible, your intuition is real, and you already carry the answers within you.

⊕ www.igniteandglow.biz
▶ www.youtube.com/@intuitiveangelreadings
❋ www.facebook.com/mysticsoulvisionspsychicmedium

Scan the QR code to learn more about Melissa.

chapter 09

They Never Stopped Talking
by Meg Evans-Blair

They Never Stopped Talking

I have always heard Spirit, for as long as I can remember! As a young girl, they would access my dreamscape and give me horrific dreams.

I would say things that would make my Mum look at me with curiosity. She would ask me things like, "Where did you learn that word?" or "Who told you that?" or "How on earth did you know that?" I would tell her that I just heard it in my head, and she, in her motherly way, would say I had a very active imagination or ask me, "Is this another one of your stories?" Until it got to the point that she had said one day, "Enough Meg, people don't like it when you tell lies."

Lies, I thought to my seven-year-old self — I wasn't lying. This was information I was being given, yet the one person in my world who my life was centred around was telling me they were lies. I was shattered.

It didn't stop the night terrors, though. Didn't stop them talking to me. Didn't stop them visiting me... so I kept it all to myself. The moments I felt people sitting on my bed, the conversations I would have with them, and the details they would tell me of other people's lives.

I became less talkative around adults and contented myself with playing dolls with my spirited friends. I still had the recurring dream of the dead people floating in the water that had a big grey wall that stopped them from getting air or escaping their surroundings. I would run screaming and crying to my parents' bed only to be told to take my dolly and go back to my own bed. Crying, I would return to the room I shared with my older sister and crawl in beside her, trying to hold back the tears and go back to sleep, way too terrified to get back in my own bed. Maybe she could stop them from happening!

For the most part I was a reasonably happy kid with a huge unfounded fear of water, which wasn't a problem because we lived three or four hours from the coast, until my Dad bought a boat. It arrived parked on its trailer and was kept on the showroom floor of my parents' motor dealership. Dad picked me up and put me on the deck of this thing and asked me if I was scared. "No Daddy," I said confidently because it wasn't moving. It was strange being up there. I had seen boats in pictures but this was weird. It wasn't even in water... How is this a boat? I was soon to find out. There was a local lake and that's where we were to spend every spare weekend.

Guess what? They put that thing in the water, the sail caught the wind, the boat tilted, the water started to come up through the gunnels and that was it. I screamed, I cried, I was terrified. This would be my life off and on for the next twelve years. Of course, the boats changed over the years from a 6-metre (20') trailer-sailer called Aquilla to a 10.5-metre (32') sloop called Peter Robyn. That yacht was my nemesis. For the most part I hated it, I hated sailing and I hated race day even more!

By this stage I was eight and a half and we had moved from Scone to Lemon Tree Passage (yes, it's a real place) and the yacht was kept on a mooring in the Passage. The kids at the school were horrible and there was no escape from the bullying. I was teased and taunted for being sensitive... I didn't even know what that word meant but I guessed it wasn't good, and was also given a hard time just because I wasn't born into their small community.

My coping mechanism was to sing. I had essentially told Spirit to stop talking to me. I didn't like being branded a liar, so I just told them to leave me alone. I knew they had stopped talking but I knew they were still there. I would hear my name and go to my Mum or Dad and ask them what they wanted. The response was always the same. No one had called my name. They were back or checking in to gauge whether I could hear them or not.

Then, they started to play music in my head. I could hear all the instruments, the words, the timing, everything. I decided to join in and sang every note and word to the songs they would insert in my head for me to listen to. I became known by the older members of the community as the little girl who sings. Didn't make any difference to my school life though, my peers either ignored me or teased me depending on their mood of the day.

There was one girl and her younger brother who had moved to the area with her parents from Sydney. In her I found a friend. We would meet on the way to school and would ride our bikes to school together, and by the time my ninth birthday came around we were firm friends. We would spend weekends together being kids. Playing, bushwalking on their property, swimming at the beach, sleepovers, all the normal kid things. Life felt great.

The morning of my ninth birthday was a school day and I met my friend and her brother on the way to school as was our morning school routine. We were riding down the hill to school one morning and a ginger cat tried to cross my path. I swerved to miss it. I tumbled over the handlebars of my bike and hit the road forehead first, right cheek then mouth. It was a horrifying accident.

I remember trying to stand up, I fell back down. I called out to my friend. She wasn't there. I couldn't see for all the blood that was now covering my eyes and soaking my school uniform. I couldn't stand up for blood loss. I crawled across the road down the gully, that acted as a stormwater drain, across the lawn of the nearest house and scratched at the door.

The locals called him Old Tom; he answered the door and immediately called out to his wife to get a towel. She must have sensed the urgency of his voice, the next thing I remember I had a towel on my head, something odd was happening. "You'll be alright now," the voice said. I passed out.

I came back around at random times throughout the whole ordeal. I remember Old Tom picking me up and carrying me almost a block to the nearest house. He took me to the closest house that had a car. Old Tom left me with Reg and his wife. Reg fired up the old Holden Special that they had, his wife sat with me, while Old Tom went up the rest of the hill to my parents' house and came back with my Mum. No mobile phones or landlines, no ambulance, and a hospital that was almost an hour away.

I came back to consciousness in my mother's arms, slowly bleeding to death on our way to the local doctor's surgery who had taken one look at me and directed them to rush to Mater Hospital in Newcastle only to lose consciousness. I have vague recollections of my uniform being cut off me and getting prepped for surgery. I don't know how long the surgery went for or for how long I was unconscious, but I woke up with a rotten headache with stitches all over my face into my hairline and just beyond! Dr James Holley, plastic surgeon, did a spectacular job!

Weeks passed and I learnt that people go to die in hospitals... they were everywhere! And they all talked or just looked at me... that, at nine, was too much! I couldn't say anything to Mum, that sort of thing was frowned upon. In Mum's world, they didn't exist, and I had an overactive imagination.

I spent days feeling terrified until she was there, somehow, I felt protected while she spent as many days as she could in there with me. She would arrive after she had dropped Dad off to work and when the time came to leave, I would cry and beg her not to. Poor Mum. It seemed like I was in there for eternity and eventually I was discharged. I went back to school only to be faced with new taunts. Scarface was their favourite.

At thirteen I decided smoking would be a good idea. Maybe that would allow me to be part of the 'in' crowd with the kids up the back of the bus. I craftily sneaked a packet of Dad's Benson & Hedges, along with a packet of matches, and headed to a secluded spot on the shores of Tilligerry Creek.

I took that first cigarette out of the packet, put it to my lips and held it in place while I got a match out to strike it. I struck the match, a sudden wind came up and blew it out! Humph, I thought... that was strange. So, I tried again. Again, that same sudden breeze came and blew out my freshly lit match. I wasn't even getting the match to the cigarette before it was extinguished by unseen forces.

"Stop it!!" I yelled at the sky. "I know what you're doing and it won't work. I want to smoke and I want to be popular!!"

They stopped blowing out my matches. And the smoking era had begun.

High school was pretty much the same with random crazy stuff happening, interjected with a library to research who I was and what I had (like I had a disease), boyfriends and learning the guitar. It seemed the older I got the more Spirit would make themselves known, mostly when I was alone or under stress. People who bullied me at school; they would either trip over just after and hurt themselves or get bleeding noses, or their car would get a flat tyre in senior years.

Yes, once or twice you could probably shrug it off or put it down to coincidence but it gets to the point that you eventually need to ask yourself the question of, how many times does something have to happen before it's mathematically impossible?

I was to learn that I have a pretty kick-arse Guardian Angel who has been protecting me, and was probably responsible for blowing out my matches, and helping me out of sticky situations for as long as I can remember.

Like the Good Friday of 1984, I was nineteen years of age and living out of home and it was decided that we (the current boyfriend, his mate and I) would go fishing to catch fish for Good Friday. The day was gloriously sunny and warm enough for the beginning of autumn and the fishing trip went well until the return journey.

A green Valiant Rambler crossed our path and stopped part way across the intersection on Nelson Bay Road (at the T-intersection that led down to Anna Bay which is now a roundabout) and the EA Ford that I was travelling in smashed into the side of the car. The driver of the green car had given us 33 metres stopping distance before we hit and at 100 kilometres an hour, it's not much stopping room.

I remember the boyfriend of the time saying, "Hold on," the driver saying, "Oh shit," and seeing the jungle green colour of the car.

I came to somehow be on the floor of our car wedged between the back seat with my right knee caught in the metal springs in the back of the front passenger's seat, part of my butt on the hump in the floor where the camshaft sits under the car and the other half almost on the floor. I really didn't feel any pain. This was amazing to me. How could I go through that and still be alive uninjured? Or at least that's what I thought at the time.

I tried to move. Nope I was stuck. Someone ran over to the car to ask if I was okay. I told them I thought I was okay; I was just stuck, and I couldn't figure out how to get out. Movement proved futile and very painful and then I blacked out.

I remember gaining consciousness. Someone asked me if I wanted anything, I responded with I wouldn't mind a cigarette, the answer was a no. Apparently fuel had spilled all over the road and everyone was being cleared from the scene in case the car I was in decided to burst into flames. I spent four hours wedged in the car going in and out of consciousness. Police Rescue was called to cut me out of the car. The police later informed me that there wasn't one straight panel left on our car and I was told by the police officer who did my follow-up statement that I was lucky my seatbelt failed because I wouldn't have survived! The lady officer had even said to me that I must have a Guardian Angel looking after me.

Over the years I've experienced so many paranormal situations each with their own individual story. They have saved me from a domestic violence attack from a physically abusive spouse through Spirit intervention and coming to my aid by creating books to go flying across the room at my assailant. Televisions have come on and off, of their own accord; and this is before the days of putting a TV on standby and using a remote to turn it off and on; light switches going off and on; knowing the correct answers to multiple choice school tests; saying what window would be chosen for the storytelling on

Play School, a popular children's TV show; I would 'guess' the letter of the day on Sesame Street; Holland blinds going up and down; stereo system lid lifting itself up and slamming down as a teen; and more recently, computer terminals refusing to work at banks until I move away; and shopping centre registers that suddenly stop working; songs coming on as messages from loved ones; 'Happy Birthday' from Tom Jones, one of my Dad's favourite singers, synchronistically played on the radio station we were listening to as we were going to celebrate my birthday with all the kids; a new car arriving on my birthday; our house being reduced $70K from original asking price the same day the home loan was approved with exactly the right amount of money being approved; to the point of wishing I was invisible only to go to vote at a Federal election to be told I wasn't on the electoral roll; or not finding my original licence at the RTA when I went to renew my driver's licence; knowing when two of my children needed specialist hospital care — one with appendicitis and the other with hepatic cholestasis — the list of events isn't endless but it certainly is extensive.

My Guardian Angel and Spirit Guides have always had a way of helping me, showing me situations in my own life either through repetitive signs, thoughts, synchronicities, animal communications or just plain talking to me.

I remember being scared to drive home on this particular afternoon. I had lessons to learn and this one of them came in the form of an abusive, now ex-spouse. As I drove closer and closer to my home I heard that familiar voice. "Don't worry Meg, he'll be gone soon and you'll be okay." Those words were so comforting. But, also more than that. Those words gave me the strength and courage to go and face my demons.

They were right. At the end of it all my baby son and I were safe. And he was gone.

Life moved on. I went back to my modelling career and had three more wonderful children. Spirit would line up incredible jobs on the fashion runway, TV commercials, short and long form films and movies, as well as print material for brochures, newspapers and more.

And then it happened.

I was on pause, my world had been turned upside down and even though everyone in the community thought my life looked peachy keen, I was desperately unhappy. My home life was volatile and controlling and now I had been diagnosed with pancreatitis. An autoimmune disease that threatened to take my life. The pain of an attack was unbearable and its persistence saw me drop weight to a staggering 41kg. That amount of weight loss on my 5'7" frame looked awful. I was a shadow of who I had been and no longer strong enough to go to auditions in Sydney or even stay awake a whole day.

I had this disease for many years, and with each passing day I would lose more weight. I had four beautiful children and my pancreas was deteriorating. My specialist gastroenterologist, Dr Radvan, had informed me that two of the three parts of my pancreas had necrosis of the tissue. Effectively my pancreas had checked out and the only part left helping me digest food and regulate my blood sugars was the head of the pancreas.

My dearest friend for the past forty years, who just happens to be a registered nurse, compiled a dossier on my disease, explaining possible causes, copying case studies from the nurses' library, showing mortality rates, treatment strategies and dietary recommendations. I studied it. I screamed. I shouted. I didn't fit any of their known categories or reasons for having this horror. I wasn't a man, I didn't have a history of alcohol abuse, I didn't come from a Mediterranean country and change my eating habits.

So WHY????

And then I found the book *You Can Heal Your Life* by Louise L. Hay.

I looked up pancreatitis and my whole understanding changed!!

I had caused this disease.

My home life, my internal dialogue, my thoughts of being insignificant and unwanted had caused this disease.

This time in my life was to become one of the biggest spiritual learning periods I have experienced. Over this time I explored more esoteric metaphysical areas that interested me. I learnt about crystals, crystal healing and pendulums. I discovered chakras, Ayurvedic treatments and meditation. I discovered colour therapy, candle magic along with the Wheel of the Year. I trained as a Reiki Master to try and heal myself. I figured if my thoughts and feelings could create this monster then I could kill it!!

I read dozens of books on self-healing. Doreen Virtue's *Healing with the Angels* oracle cards were all the rage offering a new and exciting way of connecting to the divine. So I bought deck after deck of hers and others. I spent hours meditating and thanking Spirit for taking my pain and making me whole again. I nurtured my body with Reiki and clean foods. I spent every waking hour researching Tarot, how to do readings, using them as a focus tool to disassociate and connect stronger with my guides.

I began to love myself again and slowly I healed.

Over time my relationship with the father of the younger three children had dissolved. And I had started my new occupation as a business owner and freelance beautician.

But, my guides had a surprise in store.

Spirit was also to bring new love into my life in the form of my now husband. I didn't know it at the time, but they were manipulating the cosmos to bring about a situation that caused me to rethink my whole life story.

I would see his name on street signs, businesses or I would hear 'Starry, Starry Night' or my eyes would be drawn to see his initials on licence plates as I would travel the freeway. I didn't actually know this at the time. I just couldn't figure out why I was seeing VLB plates wherever I went.

Spirit even had the ability to have several women call out his name

THE SOUL'S RISING

during a name game at a baby shower I attended. All the signs, all the synchronicities, all the little nudges somehow came to a head not long after my father passed on 5.5.05. Change was imminent.

And the experiences continue...

Meg Evans-Blair

Meg Evans-Blair, known professionally as Mystic Meg, is a celebrated Psychic, Medium, and Spiritual Guide renowned for compassionate, insightful guidance. She harmonises Tarot, Oracle cards, and energy reading to help individuals connect with their higher selves, loved ones in spirit, and their true purpose.

A prolific creator, Meg co-authored a number of oracle decks, authored a transformative book on awakening and intuition, and developed empowering affirmation cards.

Her work centres on elevating vibrations, manifesting dreams, and nurturing ongoing spiritual growth, while fostering heartfelt connections with those who have crossed over. Through readings, practical tools, and teachings, she inspires a global community of seekers to awaken their innate psychic gifts and live authentically in alignment with their highest good.

Mystic Meg's soulful approach invites clarity, trust, and real-world applications, guiding people to embrace their gifts, deepen their spiritual practices, and live with intention, compassion, and radiant inner light.

🌐 www.mysticmegpsychicmedium.com.au
👍 www.facebook.com/share/1717QPBBMc
📷 www.instagram.com/mysticmeg181

Scan the QR code to learn more about Meg.

chapter 10

Crisis as Catalyst: When Love Became the Initiation

by Joergette Mae Medel

Crisis as Catalyst: When Love Became the Initiation

I never imagined that crisis could be a catalyst for awakening. For most of my life, I believed crisis meant failure — that if something fell apart, it was because I had done something wrong. I thought I had loved incorrectly, missed a lesson, or broken an invisible rule I was supposed to follow. To me, crisis meant loss, shame, and the end of something sacred. It was proof that I hadn't been enough — not patient enough, devoted enough, or resilient enough. I had internalised the belief that if life unravelled, it was because I had failed to hold it together.

I believed love, when done properly, should be stable, predictable, and contained. I believed devotion was proven through endurance, through staying, and through surviving discomfort quietly and calling it commitment. If something ended, surely it meant I hadn't tried hard enough or sacrificed enough of myself to make it work.

That belief system shaped how I loved, how I stayed, and how I endured. It explained away the quiet ache in my chest that whispered something isn't right here, even when everything looked fine from the outside. So, when my marriage began to unravel, it didn't just break my heart; it fractured my world view. The unravelling itself, and the love journey that followed, didn't arrive gently. It arrived honestly, revealing a truth I hadn't been ready to see before: sometimes life doesn't fall apart to punish us; sometimes it falls apart to wake us up.

For a long time, I lived inside a version of love that looked right from the outside. It was responsible, respectable, and predictable. I was doing what I believed love required of me — being loyal, committed, accommodating, and reliable. I wore the roles well: wife, mother, daughter. I showed up, I met expectations, and I kept the peace. I held everything together, sacrificing quietly and calling it love.

I had become very good at being needed — the ultimate people-pleaser. I was dependable and skilled at reading the emotional weather of others, adjusting myself accordingly. I learned how to sense when someone was uncomfortable before they even named it; how to soften my edges, anticipate needs, and make myself easier to be with. What I didn't realise then was that this constant self-adjustment was slowly costing me my own aliveness.

Something in me was dimming, but I didn't have the language for it. I couldn't name it without guilt rising in my chest. To acknowledge it felt disloyal, ungrateful, and selfish. I had been taught that love meant putting others first, and I had taken that teaching all the way to self-erasure. Somewhere along the way, I learned to measure love by how much of myself I was willing to give up. I learned to stay small to stay safe, to soften my truth to avoid conflict, and to confuse endurance with devotion. I mistook consistency for connection, stability for intimacy, and sacrifice for love. I was present in my life, but I wasn't fully alive within it.

Looking back now, I can see how disconnected I had become from my own soul. I had learned to love from obligation rather than alignment — from fear rather than truth. I was loyal to the roles I played, but disconnected from the woman playing them. I knew how to show up for everyone else; I just didn't know how to show up for myself without apology.

So, when the words, "I want a separation," entered my world, they shattered more than the structure of my marriage. They shattered the identity I had built my safety upon: the version of me who believed being chosen meant being worthy, who believed security came from someone else staying, and who believed love could be earned through self-sacrifice.

I remember the silence that followed those words. The way time seemed to slow and speed up all at once. The tightness in my chest, the ringing in my ears, and the sensation that the ground beneath me had disappeared. I remember wondering how something that had once felt so solid could dissolve so quickly. My mind raced ahead to logistics — what would need to be managed, held together, and explained; how the pieces might be rearranged and how to minimise disruption. But

Crisis as Catalyst: When Love Became the Initiation

beneath that mental noise lived a quieter, more devastating question: "If this is ending... who am I now?".

That moment was a crisis, but it was also the first crack. In the stillness that followed the separation, I came face-to-face with myself in a way I never had before. Without the familiar roles to hide behind and without the constant motion of keeping everything afloat, there was nowhere to perform, nowhere to disappear, and nowhere to redirect my energy outward. I had to listen. What I heard, quiet at first, was my own soul calling me home. It whispered that the pain wasn't here to destroy me; it was here to reveal me.

Grief became my teacher. Fear became my mirror. Loneliness became an initiation. I stopped trying to rush my healing or force meaning onto the pain. I stopped asking, "How do I fix this?", and began asking, "What is this trying to show me?".

There were days when the grief felt bottomless and nights when the quiet was so loud it pressed against my ribs. There were moments when my nervous system felt raw and unprotected, as though everything familiar had been stripped away. I began to notice how much of my identity had been shaped around holding everything together. Without the familiar structure of partnership, there was an unsettling spaciousness — a quiet that didn't ask anything of me, yet revealed everything.

I realised how often I had used busyness as a way to avoid myself; how productivity had become a form of self-worth and how being needed had quietly replaced being known. Healing did not move in a straight line; it spiralled, revisited, and deepened. Grief returned unexpectedly at times, sharp and insistent, reminding me that letting go is not something we complete, but something we practise. I learned that grief is not something to resolve, but something to listen to. Each wave carried information, pointing to a place where I had once abandoned myself in order to belong.

I also began to feel the difference between being alone and being lonely. Alone was spacious. Lonely was the ache of having been disconnected from myself long before I was disconnected from another. For the first time in a long time, I wasn't performing strength or managing perception. I wasn't holding a shape that no longer fit.

I journalled through tears that felt endless and sat in meditation with unanswered questions and a nervous system that didn't yet know how to rest. I learned what it meant to surrender — not as weakness, but as radical honesty. I learned how to sit with discomfort without abandoning myself, and how to stay present when everything in me wanted to escape. This was the beginning of my return. Not dramatic or instant, but quiet, gradual, and deep. I realised I wasn't searching for another partner; I was reclaiming myself.

In reclaiming myself, I realised how little I actually knew about who I was outside of my roles. So much of my adult life had been shaped around responsibility and expectation that my own desires had slowly faded into the background. I began to turn my attention toward myself with curiosity rather than criticism: "What do I enjoy now?", "What lights me up when no one is watching?", "What parts of me did I quietly abandon because they didn't fit the life I was living?".

I started unlearning the conditioning that told me joy was frivolous, that rest had to be earned, and that pleasure needed to be justified. I questioned the narratives I had inherited about what a 'good woman' prioritises and how much space she is allowed to take up. I let myself do things simply because they felt good. I returned to interests I had once loved and then quietly set aside — things that made me feel expressive, creative, and alive. I noticed how my body responded when I gave myself permission to enjoy rather than endure. There was a softness that returned; a spark; a remembering. This wasn't indulgence; it was integration.

I also noticed how my social world was shifting. I felt a growing disconnect from old friendships that revolved around shared roles I no longer inhabited in the same way. Being around married friends with children sometimes amplified the sense that I was in-between identities — no longer who I was, not yet who I was becoming. So, I allowed myself to create new connections. I spent time with people who met me in this version of myself — not the role I had played, but the woman I was becoming. Conversations felt lighter, more spacious, and more rooted in presence. This didn't mean I rejected my past; it meant I honoured where I was now.

In choosing new environments, new rhythms, and new expressions of myself, something quietly stabilised inside me. I wasn't waiting to be reattached to feel whole; I was learning how to belong to myself.

As this belonging deepened, my patterns began to reveal themselves with greater clarity. I saw how often I had given parts of myself away in exchange for certainty; how often I had overridden my intuition to keep the peace; how often I had mistaken attachment for love and endurance for devotion. I began to understand that my nervous system had learned to equate familiarity with safety — even when that familiarity came at the cost of my truth. What felt logical was often just what was known.

I noticed how quickly my body sought reassurance and how instinctively it scanned for cues of approval. How easily it mistook emotional intensity for connection. My breath would shallow in moments of uncertainty; my chest would tighten when I sensed distance. The impulse to move toward rather than pause, to soothe rather than stay, was deeply ingrained. This wasn't a flaw; it was a learned survival strategy.

And once I could see it without shame, something softened. I stopped trying to override my responses and began to listen to them. I treated my nervous system like a younger part of me that had learned how to cope in the best way it knew how. Instead of demanding that I be healed or resolved, I offered myself patience. I learned that safety doesn't come from predictability; it comes from presence — from knowing I can meet myself honestly in whatever arises.

This deeper trust followed me into my next partnership. When we came together, it wasn't neat or conventional. There was deep connection, resonance, and truth — and also uncertainty. He wasn't quite ready to be exclusive, and that uncertainty stirred something deep within me. Old wounds surfaced and old fears spoke loudly. The familiar ache of not being chosen tightened around my chest. "Why am I not enough? What do I need to do to be chosen?"

This time, the crisis wasn't external. It was internal. I could feel myself standing at a crossroads I knew intimately. One path invited me to grasp, to control, or to exit before I could be hurt and call it strength — to choose distance over depth and name it self-preservation. It was the logical choice, the one that promised safety through withdrawal rather than truth. That path was familiar; it had kept me safe before.

The other path asked something far more terrifying. It wasn't logical, neat, or guaranteed. It asked me to stay — not attached or hopeful, but present. Not because it made sense, but because it felt true. This was the initiation: not into partnership, but into self-trust.

The choice did not happen once. It happened again and again in small moments: when I felt the urge to ask for reassurance and chose instead to breathe; when I noticed the impulse to over-explain and allowed silence to hold; when fear rose and I chose not to collapse into old stories about inadequacy. Each moment became a practice; each pause became a threshold. I wasn't suppressing my needs; I was learning to distinguish between needs that required external validation and those that invited deeper internal anchoring.

This wasn't detachment; it was intimacy with myself. From that place, I could meet him honestly, without agenda, bargaining, or shrinking. For the first time, I was staying open without self-betrayal. I saw that we were both seeking the same thing: unconditional love. Not love rooted in fear or ownership, but love that allows space, honours choice, and tells the truth. I saw, with undeniable clarity, that if I wanted to receive that kind of love, I had to embody it first.

So, I stopped trying to secure love from outside myself. I stopped negotiating my worth or asking another to reassure what I was unwilling to anchor within. Instead, I turned inward. I met my insecurities with compassion rather than judgment. I learned how to sit with the part of me that feared abandonment and say, "I'm here." I stopped performing worthiness and started embodying it. I chose honesty over reassurance, presence over protection, and truth over the illusion of safety.

I chose to love without manipulation, expectation, or strategy — not because it guaranteed an outcome, but because it kept me whole. As I rooted more deeply into myself, clarity emerged between us. Not through pressure, but through presence and integrity. Through the freedom to choose rather than the fear of losing.

Something subtle but unmistakable shifted. Not because I asked for clarity or tried to steer the outcome, but because I stopped interfering with truth. As I released the need to be chosen, space opened for choice to reveal itself naturally. The absence of pressure became an invitation. The steadiness of my self-trust created a different field between us — one that neither rushed nor withheld, but simply told the truth.

In that space, he came to his own realisation. Not through an ultimatum, but through resonance. He saw clearly that what he desired was a partnership rooted in presence rather than hesitation. His choice was not extracted; it was claimed. And that mattered more than anything because, this time, I was not being chosen in exchange for my self-abandonment. I was being chosen while remaining fully myself.

That distinction rewrote something ancient inside me. For so long, being chosen had felt like relief — like safety returning. But it was often accompanied by the quiet cost of self-monitoring and self-adjusting. This time, being chosen felt spacious and calm. There was no rush to secure the future or define everything; just a shared willingness to meet each other in truth. And perhaps most importantly, I knew that even if the outcome had been different, I would have been okay — not because it wouldn't hurt, but because I hadn't abandoned myself along the way.

That knowing was the real integration.

This partnership continues to be a living mirror for my healing and conscious becoming. Not because it is perfect, but because it is real. It invites me to remain awake to my triggers, my patterns, and my truth. It teaches me that love is not something to secure, but something to choose daily and consciously from a place of self-trust. As I remain anchored within myself, our connection unfolds with integrity — not through need, but through mutual presence. We meet as whole beings, not as wounds seeking completion.

This is where my understanding of love has transformed. Love is not about losing yourself to keep another; it is about staying present with yourself while opening your heart to another. Conscious partnership does not remove discomfort; it teaches us how to meet it with awareness. It does not promise certainty; it offers alignment. It does not save us from ourselves — it invites us into deeper self-responsibility.

Both the ending of my marriage and the unfolding of this partnership have served as sacred catalysts in my awakening. Together, they revealed that love, when approached consciously, is one of our greatest spiritual teachers. Love shows us where we still grasp, where we still fear, and where we are still learning to trust ourselves. Logic seeks certainty. Truth asks for courage. And love, I have learned, does not live where certainty is demanded, but where truth is honoured.

If you find yourself in the midst of a transition — relational or otherwise — that is stirring discomfort or deep emotion, know this: something within you is not broken. Something within you is seeking to become visible.

Crisis does not arrive to punish us for getting it wrong. It arrives as a catalyst — a turning point in our evolution. It is a moment when the structures that once kept us safe can no longer contain who we are becoming. Crisis enters when growth can no longer be postponed, when the soul requires movement, and when transformation is no longer optional. What cracks in these moments is rarely the relationship alone; what cracks is the identity that required self-abandonment to survive.

Logic will tell you to protect yourself, to retreat, and to choose certainty at any cost. Logic wants guarantees and timelines. But truth asks something different. Truth asks you to stay present, to listen beneath the noise of fear, and to choose integrity over armour.

This is the threshold most of us were never taught how to cross: the place where safety and truth no longer point in the same direction. It is the place where love stops being about being chosen and becomes about choosing yourself first.

Sometimes a heart must crack before it can open fully. Sometimes the life you built must loosen its grip so the life that fits can find you. When crisis becomes a catalyst, love is no longer something you bargain for; it becomes something you meet consciously. This is what crisis ultimately offers us: not devastation, but initiation. Not punishment, but evolution.

It is an invitation to live more truthfully and love more honestly — to allow what is false to fall away so what is real can finally take shape. And when we answer that invitation, love changes shape. It stops asking us to disappear. It asks us to arrive. Fully. Truthfully. As we are.

Joergette Mae Medel

Joergette Mae Medel is a Soul Purpose Activator, Intuitive Guide, International Speaker, and Soul Coach devoted to supporting women through life's pivotal turning points. Her work bridges spirituality, trauma-informed awareness, and conscious leadership, offering a grounded, heart-led approach to awakening, purpose, and embodied living.

Shaped by profound life transitions including separation, identity loss, and spiritual initiation, Joergette discovered a powerful truth: crisis is not an ending, but a catalyst. Through the unravelling of her former life, her soul's work emerged — guiding women back to self-worth, inner truth, and self-trust.

Known for weaving depth with practicality, she supports women who feel torn between responsibility and purpose to consciously create lives aligned with their values and inner truth. A mama of four and homeschooling parent, she embodies integration over balance. In The Soul's Rising, Joergette shares a deeply personal chapter that reveals crisis as a catalyst for awakening, transformation, and evolution through conscious love, separation, and self-choice.

❶ www.facebook.com/joergettemaeemedel/
◉ www.instagram.com/joergettemaemedel/
❽ www.beacons.ai/joergettemaemedel/

Scan the QR code to learn more about Joergette.

chapter 11

The Woman with Wings She Didn't Know She Had

by Liz Mulheron

The Woman with Wings She Didn't Know She Had

I didn't wake up one day knowing who I was meant to become. There was no lightning bolt, no single moment of revelation — only a slow unfolding, shaped by grief, devotion, love and loss. For much of my life, I didn't know I had wings at all. I only knew what it felt like to be cracked open by experience, to be brought to my knees by circumstances I didn't choose, and to keep walking anyway. It was through those moments — the ones that broke me, stretched me and demanded everything of me — that my wings were quietly forming.

I didn't grow up in a psychic household. There were no mediums or clairvoyants in the family. But my mother was a deeply devoted Catholic who prayed to God, Jesus and Mother Mary with absolute faith. She would say the Rosary, pray to Saint Jude, Saint Anthony or Mother Mary — and things happened. Miracles unfolded. So even as a young girl, I grew up knowing the divine was real, accessible and loving. All it took was asking Mum to pray, and somehow everything would work itself out.

What I didn't fully realise until much later was that my mother was a healer in her own way. She was a nurse, and while she would never have called herself 'intuitive' or 'psychic,' she healed through compassion, prayer and presence — the same qualities I now use in my work, just expressed differently. I can see now how deeply I took after her.

Life taught me early that change is natural and often arrives uninvited. When I was six, my father underwent open-heart surgery and was told he had only three months to live. Thankfully, he lived for another six years, passing away when I was twelve; he was only fifty-nine.

What I find interesting is that I don't hold many clear memories of my dad. After his surgery, he was unable to work, so he was home for much of my childhood — yet my strongest bond was always with my mother. Looking back now, through the lens of the intuitive person

I've become, I sense that even as a child I somehow knew who would be around for the long term. Perhaps that quiet knowing is why I gravitated so deeply toward her.

When Dad passed, Mum had very little money and returned to full-time work as a nurse. She never complained, never cried, never showed anger; she simply carried on. And as a young child, I just knew everything would be okay. I don't know how I knew, but I did. Mum had her faith, and looking back now, I see that this was where she learned to trust the unseen. That trust carried her forward, and it carried me too.

I was the equal youngest of ten children. I had a twin brother, born fifteen minutes after me, making him number ten and me number nine, while my eldest sister was fifteen years older than us. When Dad died, the impact rippled through our family in very different ways. Each of us grieved according to our age, our role and our understanding of loss. Some carried responsibility too soon, others carried silence, and some carried heartbreak they didn't yet have words for.

For me, it was chaotic, painful and overwhelming. Yet within that chaos, something else was formed. I learned resilience, adaptability and the quiet strength that comes from surviving life's most difficult chapters; long before I understood what those qualities were.

Pain struck again in my early teens when my brother David, who was two years older than me, was hit by a car while coming home from school. Thankfully, he wasn't seriously injured, but during the medical examinations doctors discovered a hole in his heart, requiring urgent open-heart surgery. As a family, we endured the fear and pain that came with it, while also supporting David through his long healing journey.

Years later, after David turned twenty-one, he travelled through Queensland. When he returned, he complained of what seemed like a simple toothache. By the time doctors realised the toothache was caused by an infection, it had already spread. The infection affected his heart, entered his bloodstream and led to massive organ failure.

Over the course of a month, I watched a fit, healthy, extraordinary young man slowly fade away. David went from vibrant and full of life to fighting for every breath. He celebrated his twenty-second birthday only days before he passed away.

The lesson for me was a profound one: life is fragile, love is never guaranteed time, and presence matters more than anything. His death taught me to feel deeply, to love without holding back, and to understand that grief is not something to 'get over' — but something that reshapes you, opening your heart in ways you never expect.

Fifteen years later, my eldest brother Ken died suddenly from a heart attack. He was a deeply happy, devoted husband and father to four young sons. After Dad's passing, Ken had quietly stepped into that role for me — the one I would call for support, reassurance and guidance. And once again, he was taken without warning.

Grief was no longer a single event in my life. It became a teacher I would meet again and again.

That teacher returned once more when my mother passed away. I was blessed that she lived a long, healthy life, dying at ninety-three. She had been my anchor, my constant source of strength, and losing her felt like the ground shifting beneath me. In her passing, she took her place beside my father and my two brothers once again.

I learned that loss can either close your heart or carve it open. Mine chose to open.

Years later, another defining chapter unfolded through my twin brother.

My twin — a beautiful, gentle soul — went through a devastating relationship breakdown. His children moved to Queensland, and the emotional stress triggered a mental health crisis, so he began smoking marijuana to cope. Soon he started seeing and hearing things that terrified him. He was diagnosed with schizophrenia and admitted to a mental institution.

He spent many years heavily medicated — so medicated that I used to call him "a lost soul," because the light in him was so dimmed. He had wonderful social workers supporting him, but his quality of life was heartbreaking to witness.

So when I later began seeing and hearing things as part of my spiritual awakening, I didn't dare tell my family. I was terrified they would think I was heading down the same path. Instead, I turned to spiritual teachers and healers who could help me understand what was happening. I followed their guidance, I followed my visions, and I honestly believe it saved me. It helped me differentiate between fear and intuition, between illness and awakening, between confusion and divine connection.

My twin brother passed away twelve months after my mother — a loss that still touches me deeply. Mum used to say she had to live to a hundred because if she did, she would outlast Chris. She felt he needed her support. But when Chris suddenly passed away from a heart attack, I truly believe it was Mum's divine intervention. She knew that if Chris had lived a long life — he was a heavy smoker — he might have ended up dependent on me, adding to the responsibility I already carried for his daughter, who lived with me along with her two young children. I believe Mum chose to take him with her to Heaven.

Yet within that profound loss came an unexpected gift. When I later channelled Chris, he told me he was free. He spoke of the colours where he now was — vivid, beautiful and filled with light, a space without pain, confusion or heaviness. He was free at last.

It was the first time in years that I felt him at peace. I told him to go and enjoy the colours and give Mum, Dad, David and Ken a hug from me — and then he was gone.

Earth isn't always where we experience freedom — but the soul always finds its way back to the light.

After experiencing the deaths of both my parents and three siblings, including my twin brother, grief became woven into the fabric of my life. Over time — and unfortunately through necessity — I became something of an expert, not only in how to survive my own grief, but in how to support others through theirs.

I also experienced grief through two failed marriages. The first ended when I was quite young. The second, though it did not last, gifted me three beautiful sons. Looking back now through my healing journey, I can see how unresolved grief from both relationships and family loss shaped my fear of fully committing again. When I truly loved someone, I often left — not because the love wasn't real, but because I was terrified of the pain of losing them, especially after knowing the devastation of death.

The deeper truth I've come to understand is this: love itself was never the danger. The fear was. Healing has taught me that I can love deeply—I simply had to allow myself to trust again.

My Personal Awakening

My personal awakening unfolded alongside another profound experience — motherhood. I have three sons, now twenty-four, twenty-two and twenty-one, but when they were little, my eldest son Lachlan suffered from severe eczema and allergies. He was allergic to almost everything. His skin was often covered in painful sores, and many nights I had to wrap him so he wouldn't tear his skin in his sleep. At preschool, children refused to play with him because they feared they'd "catch something." It broke my heart.

I was determined to help him before he started school. Holistic therapy became our path. I took him to a kinesiologist, and although the treatments were expensive and money was extremely tight, I made it work. I often stretched the grocery budget just to afford his sessions. But they helped — his skin improved.

My second son Trent also had significant allergies, so I went through the same process. But this time, the treatments didn't work. Eventually, the practitioners suggested his allergies and skin issues were emotional, not physical, and encouraged me to see a spiritual healer. It felt foreign and uncomfortable, but I went.

Through those sessions, it became clear that the emotional root wasn't Trent — it was the environment he was living in. My marriage had turned toxic. Leaving that relationship with three children under six was the hardest decision of my life, but within three months of leaving, Trent's skin began to clear.

The body speaks what the mind and spirit try to silence.

I continued seeing the healer not because I wanted to become one, but because I needed to understand myself. One day she handed me a flyer for a spiritual course and said, "You need to learn to do readings." I laughed, because I had no money. A few weeks later, I found myself sitting at my dining table — bills in one pile, the flyer in another, and a tax return cheque sitting on top. The cheque was the exact amount of the course.

My mother, with her unwavering faith, said, "You're meant to do this. I'll pay for the airfare."

That plane ticket was the first step toward everything I've become.

During a practice reading at the course, a man who looked very much like a free-spirited hippie said to me, "No one reads like you." I replied, "Well, that's what we're here to do," but he insisted, "Yes, but no one reads like you!" Then he added with a big smile, "I like your wings."

I laughed and asked, "What wings?"

"The ones on your shoulders," he said, still smiling.

Instinctively, I turned my head to glance over my shoulder, half expecting to see something there. At first, I thought he must be a bit eccentric — but later I realised he was sensing the angelic energy around me, something I hadn't yet learned to recognise.

From there, experiences continued — heat flowing from my hands, spontaneous energetic shifts, intuitive insights — and each time, I found the training needed to understand and use those abilities responsibly — Reiki, Pranic Healing, Mediumship and Psychic Development.

It felt as though Heaven gave me experiences, and I went out and found the education to honour them.

Then Heaven gifted me a very difficult personal lesson to learn — my own health issue: an oversized, broken heart.

A recurring theme in my family has always been heart issues. By what felt like sheer coincidence — or perhaps something more — when I was forty-eight, I discovered I had a 26mm hole in my heart, and that my heart had enlarged to nearly three times its normal size. The enlargement was caused by years of extra pressure from the hole. I required urgent surgery, or I wouldn't make fifty.

Sitting with the surgeon and my older brother Gary, I was given two options: open-heart surgery, or keyhole surgery with only a ten percent chance of success. Without hesitation, Gary said, "Let's take the ten percent." I agreed.

The fear was immense. Facing heart surgery is terrifying at any age, but even more so when I had three young boys depending on me. I prayed constantly. I asked everyone I knew to pray. I even went onto Facebook and asked for support — and people showed up. They truly did.

During the surgery, the device the surgeon inserted to close the hole held perfectly. Afterwards, he said to me, almost in disbelief, that it shouldn't have worked — but it did. I was even placed in a private room in a public hospital, which felt like a small but beautiful blessing — the icing on the cake.

I know, without doubt, that I was carried through by faith, by family, by friends, by clients, by prayer and by something far greater than luck. Divine intervention is the only way I can describe it. By following guidance, seeking help and choosing trust even when fear was loud, I was spared.

That guidance became especially profound through the presence of Archangel Michael, who supported me every step of the journey. He offered channelled words and affirmations that gave me strength and certainty — an unshakable knowing that everything would work out.

THE SOUL'S RISING

His only request of me was simple yet powerful: to share his words with the world.

And so, after my recovery, I honoured that promise by creating the Archangel Michael Empowerment Cards, which are still available today. He kept his word that I would be healed, and I kept mine — to share his message.

What I know now, with absolute certainty, is this: my role is to support others. I have many years left in this lifetime to continue healing and helping to do God's work in the way I am meant to. Over time, this calling has grown into a body of work that includes readings, healings, mediumship, intuitive mentoring and coaching.

People come to me carrying trauma, illness, grief, difficult decisions, childhood wounds or simply a desire to understand their purpose. My role is not to impress or predict. It is to help them see their path clearly and to remove the blocks that prevent them from moving forward.

If you imagine a person standing with bright sunshine before them and dark clouds behind them, it's rarely a lack of desire that keeps them still. More often, it is the invisible barriers — fear, grief, old stories, childhood trauma, unhealed wounds — that prevent them from stepping forward or releasing what no longer serves them. My role is to see the sun ahead of them, acknowledge the clouds behind them, and gently dissolve the barriers in between.

That is my calling — not born in a single moment, but shaped over a lifetime of experience that revealed the sacred nature of my work. I do not take it lightly. I honour it, I protect it, and I remain endlessly grateful for the privilege of helping others remember who they truly are.

The psychic in me sees the light that already exists within them.

The healer in me gently releases what no longer serves them.

And the channel in me brings them together, so they can move forward into the life meant for them.

My work is sacred to me. I don't take it lightly or for granted. I'm not God — I am simply the vessel through which God's work flows. I am the conduit, the bridge, the messenger.

Looking back now, I see how it all began.

With a mother who prayed with unwavering faith. A father whose early passing taught me the fragility of life and the quiet strength of resilience. Being one of ten children, learning early about family dynamics, responsibility and the many ways grief touches each of us differently. A twin brother who taught me compassion in its purest form.

Grief — my patient teacher — showed me that keeping my heart open matters. Love never dies; it simply shifts its vibration. Children who needed unconditional love, support and healing. Two marriages that ended, teaching me lessons in surrender, self-discovery and resilience. A heart that faced the brink of death and was healed, teaching me the power of trust, faith and resilience.

A life that repeatedly challenged me to grow.

Everything that once broke me became the reason I now guide others toward healing.

What Life Has Taught Me So Far

"To have the courage to follow guidance, even into the unknown — trusting that unseen support is always there, and that even in the deepest pain, love remains, life unfolds, and our hearts are stronger than we ever imagined."

"Within each of us, our hearts are born from a spark of light — the sacred place where love begins. This spark flows endlessly on its eternal journey, as infinite and as unique as you."

"You are a rare and precious gift, meant to shine. Embrace you, and never forget your worth."

Before You Turn the Page

What is life quietly teaching you?

Take a moment to look back on your life — not through the eyes of a victim, but with tenderness, compassion and an open heart. Every heartbreak, every grief, every moment that felt unbearable has been shaping you into a deeper, wiser version of yourself.

Choose faith over fear. Offer kindness as freely as you hope to receive it. Trust the quiet strength that has carried you this far, and allow yourself to shine as the beautiful soul you were always meant to be. When you do, life has a way of aligning in ways far greater than you could imagine.

And remember this, always:

You are loved more deeply than you realise.

Angel blessings,
Liz.

Liz Mulheron

With over 15 years of experience as an intuitive expert and holistic counsellor, Liz guides individuals through struggle, fear and emotional blocks to find clarity, balance and inner strength. She combines mentoring, mindfulness, energy healing, mediumship, Reiki, Pranic healing, angel intuitive and psychic work, card readings, business and life coaching to provide a deeply personalised, holistic approach.

Liz helps clients restore balance across the three key areas of life:
• Work • Family • Self

By clearing stress, anxiety, limiting habits and energetic blocks, clients unlock their true potential, creating lasting positive change for themselves and those around them.

Through spiritual insight combined with powerful healing and cleansing practices, Liz supports long-term transformation. With grace, compassion and clarity, she guides her clients through life's challenges and into a healthier, happier and more aligned way of living. Liz works with individuals seeking deep healing and lasting change.

⊕ www.lizmulheron.com
❶ www.facebook.com/emulheron
◉ www.instagram.com/elizabethmulheron

Scan the QR code to learn more about Liz.

chapter 12

When Your Soul Chooses Itself

by Michelle Wollaston

When Your Soul Chooses Itself

Awareness has always been present in my life. What changed was not its arrival, but my willingness to listen to it, and to allow it to disrupt the life I had built. For many years, I assumed awareness was something that arrived at certain moments, something you accessed when life paused long enough to let you reflect. What I later came to understand is that awareness is constant. It does not appear when you are ready. It waits while you keep negotiating with what you already know.

Long before I had language for intuition or 'inner authority', I understood what it felt like to register something beneath the surface of events. I did not experience awareness as dramatic insight or sudden revelation. It was quieter than that, more like orientation. A steady sense of direction, a way of recognising what was true before evidence caught up. I did not question it or try to interpret it. It was simply part of how I moved through the world.

My earliest conscious experiences of awareness beyond the purely physical occurred during my teenage years, in the context of my father's illness. Chronic illness reshapes a household in ways that are difficult to explain unless you have lived inside it. Time changes. Priorities shift. Conversations carry an undertone of worry, fatigue, or grief even when nobody names it directly. In our family, my father's illness did more than alter daily routines. It opened a door.

As he navigated his health challenges, my father began exploring meditation, healing work, and direct communication beyond the physical. These were not treated as belief systems or ideologies. They were practical responses to what he was living through, ways of coping, understanding, and staying present when the future felt uncertain. When the body becomes unreliable, attention becomes essential.

Spirituality was presented as part of life rather than something separate from it. It was woven into the household. Mediumship was not an idea to me; it was something I witnessed. I listened to messages attributed to loved ones who had passed, to spirit guides, and to people working consciously with what they believed to be non-physical intelligence. Alongside that, there were conversations about cause and effect, choices and consequences, responsibility, and accountability. Sometimes it was called universal law. Sometimes it was simply common sense spoken in a different language. The point was not to impress anyone. The point was to pay attention.

There was no emphasis on belief. There was emphasis on attention.

What mattered was not what someone claimed to know, but how they carried themselves while knowing it. Some people wanted reassurance. Some people wanted certainty. Others wanted answers that would remove discomfort rather than help them live with it. Early on, I learned that comfort is often mistaken for wisdom. When messages came through that carried weight, they were not dramatic. They were precise. They named what was happening and returned responsibility to the person receiving them.

At the time, I did not consider this spiritual development. That is simply how life unfolded. There was no sense of initiation or specialness attached to it. My father's illness brought the unseen closer, not as an escape from difficulty, but as a way of understanding it. What I learned early was that awareness does not remove hardship or soften reality. It sharpens perception.

I also learned something subtler, something that would matter later. Awareness does not demand immediate action. It registers. It waits. It holds information until response becomes necessary. It does not rush you, but it does not disappear.

What I did not understand then was that this period established a reference point, an internal baseline. I knew what it felt like to be internally oriented without strain, to notice without searching, to listen without urgency. That knowing did not disappear as life moved on, but it receded as other priorities took hold.

As I moved into adulthood, responsibility became the organising principle of my life. Work required focus. A long-term relationship required commitment. Parenting required constancy. Financial security requires reliability. I did not reject awareness, but I deprioritised it. I became capable, efficient, dependable. I learned how to anticipate needs, manage multiple demands, and solve problems quickly. Those skills served me well. They also trained me to override my own internal signals.

The override was not dramatic. It did not look like betrayal. It looked like practicality. It looked like being the one who stayed calm, the one who absorbed discomfort, so others did not have to. It looked like smoothing over conflict so the day could continue, adjusting myself to maintain stability, and postponing my own questions until a later time that never quite arrived.

This shift did not happen suddenly. It happened incrementally, through repetition: through choosing what was sensible over what was true, through postponing uncertainty, through minimising discomfort because other people needed stability, through telling myself there would be time later. From the outside, life appeared stable. Inside, there was a persistent sense that something important was being overruled. Awareness remained present, but it was no longer consulted. Decisions were made around it, not from it. I had stopped listening.

Over time, I began to confuse endurance with strength. If I could tolerate something, I assumed I should. If I could keep going, I assumed it would be fine. I placed quiet pride in being the one who did not fall apart, the one who kept things functioning. The cost of that pride was subtle but cumulative. It trained me to measure myself by output rather than truth. It trained me to accept the absence of joy as normal and the absence of peace as something to be managed.

I was living primarily from survival, from the need to stay steady, meet expectations, and keep things functioning. Much of my energy went into endurance rather than responsiveness. When inner cues arose, asking me to reassess or pivot, I noticed them and moved past them. Like many women, I organised my life around other people's needs and comfort, not because I lacked awareness, but because listening to it felt impractical.

This way of living produces a particular kind of exhaustion. Not the exhaustion of doing too much, but the exhaustion of holding yourself in a shape that does not fit. You can function, contribute, and even succeed while living with an inner friction that never resolves. For a long time, I assumed this was simply adulthood. I assumed the quieter parts of the self were meant to wait until everything else was managed.

But awareness does not disappear because it is ignored. It becomes background tension.

Because I was no longer listening, and because the way I was living had reached its limit, movement became necessary. This is often how spiritual or universal intervention works. It does not argue or negotiate. It creates motion. For many people, that motion arrives as collapse, what tarot practitioners call a Tower moment, the collapse of structures built on unstable ground.

That was not how intervention arrived for me.

What arrived instead was recognition. Not shock, not destruction, not a dramatic rupture that forced immediate change, but a quiet re-entry into something already known. Rather than tearing something down, it illuminated what was already unstable and made it impossible to continue pretending otherwise. It did not demand action on the spot. It made self-deception harder to maintain.

The invitation arrived quietly through my social media feed. A local event. A local medium. A modest entry fee. Nothing about it announced significance. And yet something registered. The part of me that had been overridden for years recognised the tone of the invitation immediately. It did not feel new. It felt familiar.

Years earlier, communication from beyond had been part of my everyday life. Spirit knew this. It knew I would not ignore the chance to re-enter that space through experience rather than effort. So, I attended.

The evening unfolded with a precision I recognised. Everyone in the room received a message from a loved one in spirit, and mine came last. I did not experience that as delay. I understood it as placement. I was meant to observe first.

I had encountered many mediums over the course of my life. I knew the difference between performance and precision, between vague reassurance and accurate connection. Discernment was not something I needed to develop. I already had it.

At the end of the event, there was a lucky door prize: a free private reading. I did not win. My girlfriend did. Out of everyone in the room, the free reading went to the person sitting beside me. Close enough to see clearly, but not close enough to bypass choice.

Spirit does not bypass free will. Booking and paying for my own session mattered. It marked the moment I moved from observer to participant.

The reading itself did not introduce anything foreign. It reflected what I already knew but had been negotiating with. The dynamics I had normalised were named plainly. The patterns I had minimised were described without embellishment. What occurred was recognition, and with it, the end of negotiation.

The message was unmistakable. I was not speaking my truth. I was not living honestly. I had organised my life around endurance rather than authenticity, and the cost was becoming unsustainable.

Mentorship followed naturally, not because I needed to learn how to listen, but because I needed support in acting on what I already knew. Awareness without response had become the problem. Discernment, accountability, and integration became the work.

At the same time, my long-term relationship became the testing ground for everything I was learning. The gap between what I knew internally and what I was tolerating externally became impossible to ignore. There comes a point where you can no longer be both the person who knows and the person who tolerates.

By 2019, that conflict could no longer be maintained. Leaving the relationship was not sudden or impulsive. It was the result of sustained attention and consistent practice. I had been choosing myself quietly and deliberately long before the final decision was made.

Ending a long-term relationship is rarely a single decision. It is many decisions layered over time, including the decision to stop minimising, to stop explaining away what hurts, and to stop making yourself smaller so the system can remain intact. Choosing yourself is rarely dramatic. It is often quiet, practical, and deeply unsettling.

When I finally left, it did not feel like a victory. It felt like alignment catching up with reality. Once I stopped using all my energy to maintain contradiction, I had energy available for decisions. The inner noise quietened because I was no longer fighting myself.

As my life reorganised, something else became clear. My capacity to hold space and support others did not come from becoming someone new. It came from no longer avoiding what had been put in front of me. I had spent years working in adult education and mentoring roles. Listening, reflecting, and supporting people through change was already part of my professional life. What had changed was the depth from which I was now working.

In everyday conversations, people began speaking to me about what was not working in their lives. Not because they were seeking solutions, but because something in the interaction made it possible for them to say what had been sitting just beneath the surface. The same themes surfaced repeatedly: disorientation, misalignment, and the quiet sense that something needed to change.

That is how the work took form. Not as a calling, but as consequence. Over time, those conversations became intentional. People were not asking to be fixed. They were asking to understand themselves, to make sense of why the strategies that once worked no longer did, and to find direction during transition.

This is the work I do today. I work with people who are capable, functional, and outwardly successful, yet quietly disoriented. People who are not broken, but no longer in harmony with the life they have built. My role is to help them interpret what they already know,

When Your Soul Chooses Itself

translate awareness into decision-making and timing, and support change that is honest, grounded, and sustainable.

Looking back, I do not see my life as a story of something entering or returning. I see a pattern of attention narrowing and widening, shaped by circumstance, choice, and response. Awareness was never absent. What changed was my willingness to treat it as essential rather than optional.

Soul evolution does not happen to us. It unfolds through how honestly; we listen and how willing we are to act. The soul does not ask for perfection. It asks for honesty. And when honesty becomes non-negotiable, the soul chooses itself.

What often goes unmentioned is how unsettling it can be to finally experience alignment after spending years simply enduring. We imagine that choosing ourselves will feel immediately liberating, that clarity will arrive cleanly and certainty will replace doubt. In reality, alignment removes the scaffolding that endurance relies on. It strips away familiar internal negotiations and leaves you face to face with yourself, without distraction. There is relief in that, but there is also vulnerability.

For a long time, my identity was built around being the one who could cope. When that structure loosened, I had to learn how to listen again, not just to awareness, but to the quieter signals of fatigue, desire, resistance, and grief. Awareness had always been present, but now it was no longer background information. It became the organising principle of my decisions.

This required a different relationship with time. Endurance compresses time. It teaches you to push through, to delay, to override. Alignment slows it. It asks you to stay with what is unfolding rather than rushing toward resolution. There were moments when I wanted to return to the efficiency of my old self, to rebuild something quickly so uncertainty would recede. But speed had been part of the problem. I had spent years moving quickly in directions that were not true.

What emerged instead was discernment. Not dramatic intuition or unwavering certainty, but a steadier ability to tell what fits and what does not. Discernment does not eliminate fear. It clarifies it. It reveals how often fear is used as justification to remain in familiar discomfort rather than risk honest change.

This clarity reshaped my relationships as well. Some connections deepened. Others quietly fell away. Not because of conflict or confrontation, but because the terms had changed. When you stop abandoning yourself, relationships adjust. Conversations become more honest. Silence becomes more revealing.

There is grief in that process. Grief for versions of yourself who survived by adapting. Grief for relationships built on mutual tolerance instead of real honesty. Grief for time spent believing that if you could just endure a little longer, things would eventually resolve themselves. I had to allow that grief without reading it as failure. In this context, grief was evidence that something real had ended.

As this internal reorientation continued, I noticed how often people around me were living with the same quiet friction I had normalised for years. They were not in crisis. They were functional, competent, and often outwardly successful. But beneath that competence was a sense of dislocation, a feeling that the life they were living no longer matched who they were becoming. They spoke about feeling restless without knowing why, about losing motivation for goals that had once driven them, about feeling ungrateful for wanting more when everything appeared fine.

What struck me was not the similarity of circumstances, but the similarity of language. People struggled to articulate what was wrong because nothing obvious was broken. Their discomfort did not fit neatly into narratives of failure or dissatisfaction. It was more subtle than that. It was the discomfort of misalignment, the tension that arises when awareness outpaces the structures built to contain it.

In conversations, I found myself listening in the same way I had learned to listen years earlier, not for what people said they wanted, but for what they already knew underneath their words. I was not offering solutions or direction. The conversations slowed. Questions replaced momentum. Again and again, people responded not with relief, but with recognition. They were not hearing something new; they were hearing something they already knew, spoken aloud without judgment.

This is when I understood that the work I now do was not a departure from my past, but a continuation of it. The skills I had developed in adult education, mentoring, and leadership had always been about interpretation rather than instruction. What had changed was the depth from which I was working. I was no longer helping people perform better within structures that no longer fit. I was helping them understand the signals asking them to change those structures.

Awareness, I came to see, is not inherently disruptive. What disrupts is ignoring it. Recognising and integrating awareness brings coherence. It reduces the energy spent on self-negotiation. It does not guarantee ease, but it restores integrity.

There is also an ethical dimension to this work that feels important to name. Encouraging people to 'listen to themselves' without helping them develop discernment can be destabilising. Awareness without grounding can become self-indulgence. Clarity without responsibility can become avoidance. This is why my work does not focus on awakening as an event or identity, but on integration as a practice. Listening is only the beginning. What matters is how a person responds to what they hear.

I do not position myself as someone who knows better than others. I position myself as someone who recognises the cost of not knowing yourself honestly. I am not interested in offering certainty where none exists. My goal is to help people trust their own pace, make thoughtful decisions instead of reactive ones, and understand that confusion can be a normal part of change rather than a personal failure.

When honesty became non-negotiable, my life did not become simpler. It became truer. And truth has its own complexity. It requires ongoing attention. It requires humility. It requires the willingness to

THE SOUL'S RISING

revise decisions as new information becomes available. It also offers something endurance never did — internal congruence.

Congruence is quiet. It does not announce itself. It feels like less effort rather than more confidence. It means fewer justifications and fewer apologies. It means saying no without explanation and yes without anxiety. It means living in a way that no longer requires constant self-monitoring, because you are no longer managing a split between what you know and what you do.

This is what I mean when I speak of the soul choosing itself. It is not an act of defiance or separation. It is an act of alignment. It is the moment when awareness stops being something we consult only when it is easy and becomes the guiding force in our lives.

In that sense, Soul's Rising is not about transcendence or escape. It is about evolution. It is about the gradual movement from endurance into coherence, from survival into authorship, from living in reaction to living in response. The soul does not rise by rejecting the human experience, but by inhabiting it more fully. As consciousness matures, attention becomes more honest and responsibility is reclaimed rather than delayed.

The soul does not demand perfection. It does not require constant certainty. It does not punish hesitation. What it asks for is honesty, practised over time. Honesty in recognising when something no longer fits. Honesty in acknowledging fear without allowing it to dictate every decision. Honesty in responding to awareness with responsibility rather than delay. This is how evolution occurs, not in dramatic awakenings, but in repeated, grounded choices.

When that honesty becomes non-negotiable, life begins to reorganise itself around it. Not suddenly, and not without effort, but steadily. Relationships shift. Work evolves. Identity loosens and reforms. What endures does so not only through effort, but through coherence. What falls away is not 'lost'; it has fulfilled its role.

This is not a destination. It is a way of living. Awareness continues to refine. Listening continues to deepen. Choice remains ongoing. But the internal division that once consumed so much energy begins to dissolve, replaced by a quieter steadiness.

And when that happens, the soul does not need to demand attention.

It has risen into it.

 ## *Michelle Wollaston*

Michelle Wollaston is a Life Directionist who works with people navigating emotionally complex and transitional seasons of work and life. With more than 25 years' experience across adult learning, leadership development, and vocational education, she brings a grounded, practical approach to helping individuals make sense of complexity and move forward with clarity.

Michelle has spent her career designing programs, leading teams, and working in high-pressure environments where judgment and responsibility matter. Today, her work centres on supporting people to understand what's really shaping their decisions and identify the direction, choices, and changes that genuinely require attention.

She is an Amazon best-selling author, host of the *Soul Loom* podcast, and a contributor to several publications. Her work is known for its calm authority, clear thinking, and ability to articulate what many people have been experiencing — but haven't yet been able to name.

⊕ www.michellewollaston.com
❶ www.facebook.com/michelle.wollaston.7
◉ www.instagram.com/michellewollaston/

Scan the QR code to learn more about Michelle.

www.ingramcontent.com/pod-product-compliance
Lightning Source LLC
Chambersburg PA
CBHW042126100526
44587CB00026B/4190